MICHIGAN
BEER

MICHIGAN
BEER

 A Heady History

PATTI F. SMITH

AMERICAN PALATE

Published by American Palate
A Division of The History Press
Charleston, SC
www.historypress.com

Detroit Public Library, Collection of Stephen Johnson, Library of Congress.

First published 2022

Manufactured in the United States

ISBN 9781467147491

Library of Congress Control Number: 2021949170

To all the brewers, workers and drinkers.

And especially to my late friends,
John and Michelle Nasers—we will have that drink when we meet again.

CONTENTS

ACKNOWLEDGEMENTS

This is not the book I thought it would be. I pitched this idea to my wonderful editor, John Rodrigue, in early March 2020, a week or so before libraries and other organizations closed. Because of the pandemic, it was just not possible to get access to many pictures or the permission to use them. Likewise, many of my research trips were not feasible. Nevertheless, this "pandemic book" made it to print. This would not have been possible without the help of many people.

A big thanks to my fellow Arcadia Publishing authors! Thanks to Stephen Johnson for granting me access to his amazing collection of memorabilia and knowledge of Detroit beer history. Likewise, thank you to Russ Magnaghi for responding to my many questions about Upper Peninsula beer. Thanks to Dianna Higgs Stampfler; one of these days, we will meet in person and share a beer! Please check out their books for more amazing history! Likewise, many thanks to Keith Howard for the amazing article on Kalamazoo beer.

Thank you to the libraries and historical societies that let me use the pictures you see in this book.

Thanks to Greg Haehnle and Scott Thede for maintaining the Haehnle and Sebewaing websites. You are keeping the dream alive.

Thanks to my friends who jumped in without hesitation to read and edit my work: Sarah Smalheer, Alicia Mackowiak (and thanks for saying hi to me on that first day in our chemistry class in the tenth grade), Kirk Westphal, Dr. Denise O'Brien, Joan Lowenstein, Jane Berliss-Vincent, Adrienne Meyer, Anne Ferrando-Klemet, Jim Shaw, Angie Smith, Emily Klemptner and Mike Creech. Special thanks to Kevin Nash for his amazing knowledge of Monroe and Al Frazier's Café.

Thank you to my family, especially my husband, Ken Anderson; my dad, Tim Smith; and my stepmom, Suzanne Smith, for supporting me in every sense of the word.

Thank you to all of those who went before me, especially the late Peter H. Blum, and all of the people who brewed the beer, harvested the ice, built the factories, malted the grain, waited on customers, delivered the kegs, made the barrels, balanced the books and kept the breweries safe and clean. And thanks to the families and wives who supported the brewers in myriad ways and all those who did the other millions of things that brewers have done since the beginning.

I hope I have done justice to the memories and legacies of our rich beer history in this great state.

INTRODUCTION

Like the waves that crash in the magnificent Great Lakes that surround Michigan, beer and brewing has constantly moved and evolved in the state. The first wave of brewers were the pioneers—the ones who came from Germany, Prussia, England, New York, Wisconsin and some were even born in Michigan. They started out as coopers, grocers, bookkeepers, or they were trained in their native countries as brewmasters. They brewed in their homes, saloons and brand-new brick breweries.

Then came the second wave of brewers, the hearty souls who regrouped after Prohibition. They fought through the restrictions of World War II, consolidation, mass-marketed beer, competition from breweries that could afford to ship cheap, cold beer all over. Some made it, some didn't. Some lasted a year, some five, some twenty. Many breweries haven't been heard of in decades, while other labels are still found on shelves in one form or another. These brewers' lives and backgrounds were as different as the beers they concocted, but they all had these things in common: malted grains, water, yeast, hops and the good times that come with them.

We are serious about our beer in Michigan. On April 10, 1933, Michigan ratified the Twenty-First Amendment. It was the first state to take this step toward ending Prohibition, the failed experiment.

Come along on a trip through the history of Michigan's brewers and beer as we explore, region by region, the history of brewing in our great state. While space does not allow for a mention of every brewery that existed, you will hopefully find some information about a place near your hometown, the place you would have drunk from had you lived in that day and age. Enjoy the stories contained in these pages, and may you find that many more are yet to be written.

I

THE UPPER PENINSULA

Most Michiganders know the joke about how we traded Toledo for the Upper Peninsula (and then you insert your own punchline about Ohio). No matter how one feels about our neighboring state to the south, we can agree that the Upper Peninsula (UP) is a land that features some of the most beautiful terrain in the state. The UP also boasts a beer history as unique as the pleasant peninsula itself.

Other regions in Michigan were heavily influenced by German brewers, but the UP can claim forebears from France. The French part of Canada, known as New France, encompassed the area we now call the UP. The first economy was based on furs, thanks to the great number of beavers in the area. Early French settlers also traded brandy, rum and some beer to the local Natives during these early times.

Both the colonial Americans and the French enjoyed spruce beer, a brew made of spruce that dates to the 1500s, when explorers were dying of vitamin C deficiency. The son of an Iroquois chief, Dom Agaya, advised boiling the tips of spruce, fir, cedar or other coniferous trees and then drinking the resulting tea as a treatment for this vitamin deficiency. From that spruce tea came *biere d'epinette*, or spruce beer. By the time the French settlers arrived in the UP, beer of this type was well known, as it was loaded with necessary vitamin C and was fairly easy to make. Though area Natives had the ingredients to make the brew—tips from spruce trees, syrup, yeast and water—the practice never became common among them.

The UP housed three military posts at a time when the U.S. Army saw beer as a "healthy and recreational drink," as it believed that beer consumption did not lead to the alcoholism and violence associated with hard liquor. Copper Harbor had a noncommercial brewery set up in the 1840s to supply daily rations of beer to the soldiers at Fort Wilkins. Additionally, beer produced in Detroit was then shipped to the UP, even before the discovery of copper and iron and the subsequent opening of the mines.

By the mid-1800s, the economy of the UP changed from fur trading and military outposts to copper and iron mines. In 1841, the discovery of copper deposits was revealed, followed by the discovery of iron ore three years later. These announcements led to an influx of emigrants from all over Europe. The German brewers arrived, and soon, their beer replaced spruce ale.

COPPER COUNTY

Nickolas and Catherin Voelker arrived in the late 1840s, eventually settling in Sault Ste. Marie. They took in two boarders, Joseph Clemens and Nickolas Ritz, and the three men established a small brewery. On June 26, 1850, they advertised in the *Lake Superior Journal* that their "brewery… would furnish [the community] with all articles in their line as good and on as reasonable terms as can be purchased elsewhere." This brewery, whose name is lost to the ages, operated about five or six years before the men moved to Copper County.

This region of the western UP included the communities of Eagle River, Ontonagon and Houghton. Prior to Prohibition, most UP breweries were located in Copper County. Like what happened elsewhere in the state, as immigrants began arriving in the UP, breweries began to open.

Franz Hahn came to America in 1853, landing in Eagle River. He traveled to Milwaukee, where he began brewing, and later returned to Houghton in 1859. There, he spent two years working with William Ott of the Union Brewery. Hahn and his brother began their own brewery, which saw success until a fire devastated the location in 1873. Undaunted, they rebuilt within two years, creating an extensive stone brewery with a capacity of ten thousand barrels annually. Unfortunately, the Panic of 1873, along with the fire losses, led to the suspension of their business in 1875.

A side view of Knivel Brewery (undated). *Courtesy of the Michigan Technological University Archives.*

Franz's story does not end there, however. He went on to manage the Houghton Bottle Beer Brewery, which was the first of its kind in the area, producing and bottling eight hundred barrels of beer annually. Henry Hofen's Houghton Bottle Beer Brewery began brewing by the barrel in 1876 and began bottling in 1880.

Early brewers Nickolas Voelker and Joseph Clemens both jumped back into the business. The latter opened his brewery in 1855, while the former brewed in Ontonagon County, assisted by numerous Prussian brewers and a teenager from Ohio named Michael Gitzow. In Houghton, William Holt, an emigrant from Prussian, brewed alongside a half dozen of his fellow immigrants.

As copper mining took off in the early 1860s, demand for alcohol outweighed production, such that liquor from Detroit and other places was imported. Saloons popped up early, and liquor was always available in the hotel bars, stores and taverns that dotted the landscape. Breweries in the mid-1800s included the Eagle River Brewery, which was started by a Prussian immigrant named Frank Knivel and operated from 1855 to 1910. Rockland, a mining village of around one thousand people, boasted the Biggi and Kelley Brewery in the mid-1870s.

The Union Brewery enjoyed on-site spring water, which led to particularly excellent beer that was advertised with the motto: "the beer that pleases." The Union Brewery brewed beer from 1857 to 1899, when it was sold to Bosch Brewing Company. Its main brands were Rheingold, Royal Brew, Rheingold porter and a malt tonic. These were distributed in Hancock, Calumet and South Range.

Haas

Adam Haas was born in Bavaria, Germany, in 1822. He began his career as a cabinetmaker in his native country and married Eva Lorsch. They had a son and daughter while still in Bavaria. Haas came to the United States at the age of thirty and moved directly to Houghton. First, he made his living operating boats between Portage Lake and Eagle River. He moved about ten miles away from his home but returned to Houghton in 1854 and began working as a trader of wine and liquor. In 1859, he constructed the first brewery in Houghton. The log building boasted a ten-barrel copper kettle and made porter and lager, enlarging as demand grew. In 1875, Haas acquired the stone brewery that formerly belonged to Franz Hahn, and along with this, his capacity for brewing enlarged to six thousand barrels per year. Haas served both as a commissioner of highways and the local coroner and had ten additional children with Eva.

Haas remained an active businessman until his death in 1878. The A. Haas Brewing Company soldiered on with help from Eva Haas and the couple's daughters and sons. At a time when women were denied most opportunities, four Haas daughters served on the company's board; their sons Joseph and Adolph served as president and vice-president, respectively. Using hand-blown glass bottles to distribute, the company brewed lager and Bohemian beer. By 1900, it was producing twenty-five thousand barrels annually. The family sold the brewery to a stock company in 1901, and operations ended in 1918 with state prohibition. On August 21, 1933, the beer began flowing again, as the Haas Brewing Company reopened at its original location in Houghton. Renovations and remodels made the facility one of the most contemporary breweries in the UP, and it is credited as the first in the UP to produce beer in cans.

The operation moved to Hancock in 1941, taking over the Park Brewery space, where it advertised that its "famous spring water" gave "the people the finest glass of beer they can drink, regardless of cost." Some of the

Haas. *Courtesy of the Michigan Technological University Archives.*

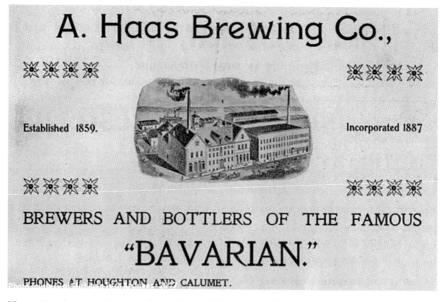

Haas advertisement. *Courtesy of the Michigan Technological University Archives.*

company's standard beers were Extra Pale Beer, Haas Bock and the generic-sounding Haas Beer.

In 1952, the name changed to Copper Country Brewing Company. Unfortunately, with increased pressure from big breweries, such as those in Detroit, Milwaukee, St. Louis and points beyond, the newly named brewery could not compete and closed in 1954.

Bosch Brewing Company

Born in Baden, Germany, in 1850, Joseph Bosch came to the United States with his parents in 1854. His father brewed in Port Washington, Wisconsin, where Joseph learned the business. A young Bosch made his trade in the industry, working at Schlitz in Milwaukee, as well as other breweries in Cleveland and Louisville. After landing in Copper County, Bosch opened Torch Lake Brewery in 1874, brewing almost two thousand barrels in his first year. The company sold mostly to saloons and boardinghouses, and it also relied on the miners working in Red Jacket (now Calumet) as its loyal customers.

The company's love of and commitment to the local area was present from the start, and it continued through the decades. Early on, Bosch sold farmers his malt and supplied them with a fresh, cold beer while they waited for their orders. More locals were brought into the business in 1876, when Bosch formed a partnership with three men and changed the company's name to Joseph Bosch & Company.

Using its artesian well water, which the company claimed benefited liver, kidney and stomach problems, the brewery flourished, brewing four thousand barrels a year by 1883. In these early days, selling bottled beer was rare in the UP, but Bosch realized the promise in this venture and started a small-scale bottling operation in 1880. By 1883, beer from about one thousand of its annual barrels was sold in glass bottles.

Tragedy struck on May 20, 1887, when a fire wiped out much of Lake Linden, taking the brewery with it. Demand for the company's beer led to a quick recovery, so it reopened in September that same year. In just over a decade, it was the largest brewery in the entire Upper Peninsula, making about sixty thousand barrels a year. In 1899, it enlarged its operations with the purchase of the old Union Brewery near Houghton.

Bosch boasted branches and storehouses in multiple locations, including Houghton, Eagle Harbor and Ishpeming. Around the same time, Joseph

Bosch billboards welcome you! *Courtesy of the Michigan Technological University Archives.*

served as the president of Lake Linden's First National Bank (which he helped organize), operated two saloons (legal in the days before Prohibition) and tended to a family that consisted of his second wife, Kate, and five children. He later served as the mayor of Lake Linden.

All the while, Joseph Bosch nurtured local connections, with advertisements touting his beer being as "refreshing as the sportsman's paradise" and using the "soft spring water" from the local spring. Pictures in the advertisements showed fishermen and skiers, tying the brand to the natural beauty and outdoor sportsmanship of the area. Other advertisements can now be seen as almost comical—like the 1903 advertisement for the company's malt tonic that says it is good "for convalescents…the weak and overworked, for nursing mothers.…Physicians recommend it."

Like almost every other brewery, Bosch struggled through Prohibition. The company placed many local advertisements pleading for temperance rather than prohibition, but eventually, it had no choice but to cease brewing alcoholic beverages. At least one advertisement shows one way the company made money: selling a brew called Bock-Edge, with an alcohol content of less than ½ percent.

After the end of Prohibition, the company began brewing beer again, focusing on its Houghton operations rather than its operations in Lake Linden. It remodeled the Scheuermann Brewery to become one of the most efficient breweries in the state.

Joseph Bosch passed away in 1937, leaving behind a legacy of service, commitment to local business and a love of brewing. After Bosch's death, Katherine Bosch (identified as his daughter in some records and granddaughter in others) and his grandsons James and Phillip Ruppe assumed control of the company. Their leadership led to increased sales and growth. This was due, at least in some part, to the incredible brand loyalty from the community and other local leaders. It became the third-largest employer in the area, peaking at 100,000 barrels of beer in 1955.

In 1965, high Michigan beer taxes, a decrease in sales and mounting competition from national brands led to talks of closing the brewery. Fortunately, all was not lost, as the community came together, gathering local executives, workers and employees, so that the family could sell to local investors. One of the key figures of this effort was Charles Finger of the International Union of United Brewery, Flour, Cereal Local 251, who served as the company's vice-president and brewmaster. Along with chief advertiser James Jeffords, Finger toured the area, rebuilding the brand's image as it spoke of the spring water and brewing techniques used by the company. The brewery promoted itself on TV and in papers, which led to an increase in sales in the late 1960s. In particular, it marketed the Light Sauna Beer, which resembled the Finnish kalja, an after-sauna beverage that is popular in Finland.

The last keg of Bosch going to Schmidt's Corner Bar. *Courtesy of the Michigan Technological University Archives.*

Despite the marketing and public appearances, sales continued to decline, and the company sold its trademarks to the Jacob Leinenkugel Brewing Company. That large brewery hired Bosch's master brewer, Vincent Charney, who continued to brew the signature brand in its traditional flavor. Even though devoted fans continued to buy and drink the product, profits eventually fell off, and Leinenkugel stopped producing Bosch in 1986.

In a ceremony on September 28, 1973, the last keg of "true" Bosch beer (brewed before the sale of the trademarks to Leinenkugel) was loaded onto a wagon and delivered to Schmidt's Corner Bar in Houghton. This last act completed the illustrious life of one of the UP's giants in the brewing industry.

Calumet Brewing Company

Once the center of the mining industry, Calumet's nickname is Copper Town, U.S.A. Its original name, Red Jacket, came from a local Native chief. In 1867, the area was incorporated as a town.

The Calumet Brewing Company began its life at 509 Pine Street as the Miswald Brothers & Company Brewery in 1898. The Miswald brothers opened their first brewery in L'Anse in 1891 and then opened another in Ontonagon four years later before settling in Red Jacket and changing the brewery's name in 1899. It was the only brewery in the town, ultimately employing almost two dozen people in 1913.

The company's slogans reflected the dietary concerns of the day. At the beginning of the twentieth century, thousands of people in England were poisoned by tainted beer. The dietary standards we enjoy today did not exist, so it makes sense that the Calumet Brewing Company's slogan included the boast that its beer was "pure and without drugs or poison." It also advised drinkers that its Wurtzburger-style beer was "recommended by physicians for sleeplessness, indigestion, and run-down systems," with the recommended dose being a glassful before meals and at bedtime.

As Prohibition looked more and more likely, Calumet Brewing Company began promoting beer as a food, as it was "nourishment…equally as wholesome as corn bread, rice pudding or barley soup." Other advertisements touted that the company's beer added "strength to both mind and muscle." Alas, Prohibition was enforced in Michigan in 1917, and with it came the closing of the brewery. It opened two years later to sell soda pop, but it was not successful.

The Calumet branch of Scheuermann Brewing Company. *Courtesy of the Michigan Technological University Archives.*

Union Brewery/Philip Scheuermann Brewing Company

In 1857, William Ault started a brewery located near freshwater springs on the Portage Canal that he called Union Brewery. After Ault passed away, Adam Youngman, Frank Maywood and Philip Scheuermann purchased the company, naming it after the latter of the trio. Scheuermann was formerly a carpenter and superintendent of a stamp mill but jumped into his new venture and brewed until he passed away in 1898. After his death, the brewery became part of the Bosch Brewing Company, and it was then renamed the Scheuermann Branch of the Bosch Brewing Company, brewing until 1918.

Park Brewing Company, Hancock

In 1906, Hancock did not have its own brewery, so a group of local businessmen aimed to change that. The original intent of the Park Brewing Company investors was to build a brewery in Houghton on the Haas Park grounds. But knowing that Hancock did not have its own brewery changed their plans. Within a few years, the company boasted ten employees. Park Brewing Company was built at East Atlantic Street and Emma Street. Its brands included Park Brew Beer, Elite Special Beer and Holiday Brew.

A Heady History

Park Brewery, circa 1910. *Courtesy of the Michigan Technological University Archives.*

The union now known as the International Union of United Brewery, Flour, Cereal and Soft Drink Workers of America was formed in 1886 to protect the work interests of the brewers, who were mostly of German descent. It was affiliated with the American Federation of Labor and went through several name changes.

In July 1913, the workers of Hancock's Park Brewing Company went on strike for better working conditions, higher wages and recognition of union membership under what was then called the International Union of United Brewery Workmen of America. They asked for a nine-hour workday, a minimum pay scale of fifteen to seventeen dollars per week and a signed working contract between the owners and the workers. When their requests were not met, ten men walked off the job. The owners quickly sent in scab workers, and production began to drop off, as locals refused to drink at saloons that carried the beer.

Charles Nickolaus, a representative of the international union's executive board, traveled to Hancock from Milwaukee on two occasions to attempt

23

A Park Brewery stock certificate. *Courtesy of the Michigan Technological University Archives.*

to reach a settlement. In the spring of 1914, the president of the brewing company asked him to come back one more time. Nickolaus returned, met with the company and a contract was signed that gave the workers what they asked for. The brewers returned to their jobs the following week. In addition to their requests, the workers obtained overtime with time-and-a-half pay. The striking workers received much support from the copper miners, who also went on strike at this time. By refusing to patronize the saloons that carried "scab beer," they rushed a settlement from management.

Like other breweries, Park had to close when Michigan approved Prohibition, but unlike many breweries, it reorganized and reopened after Prohibition's repeal. By 1937, its sales were flourishing. It was bought by Cohodas-Paoli in 1941, and the property then became part of the Haas Brewery.

MARQUETTE

A number of breweries operated in the Marquette Iron Range, situated around Ishpeming, Negaunee and Marquette. These breweries included the George C. Shelden Brewery, Ferdinand Winter Brewery and the Meeske and Hoch Brewery, all of which operated in the last decades of the nineteenth century. While little is known about these breweries, there is some information about the Upper Peninsula Brewing Company, which was founded by George Rublein, who also happened to be the first German brewer in the area. George and his wife, Catherine, arrived in Marquette via Milwaukee and purchased land on which to grow grain and hay. After amassing some personal wealth, Rublein opened a brewery on his farm. Following a fire and rebuilding, he opted to reestablish his Franklin Brewery in 1873, closer to town on property that had a natural spring running under it. Within a few years, Rubelin opened Whiteville Elysium, which included a music stand, a hall and summer homes, and it quickly became a main source of recreation for the townspeople. For the grand opening of this venture, Rublein offered free samples of his goods. Almost the entire population of the city showed up for this event; fortunately (and perhaps presciently), Rublein engaged the services of a private security force to keep things calm.

This latest operation, known as Concordia Brewery, reached a production capacity of fifteen thousand barrels while quenching Marquette's desire for beer. Despite these successes, Rublein dealt with competition and a financial panic; his brewery closed in 1878. The property passed through the hands of various owners/brewers, ultimately ending up in the hands of Meeske and Hoch, emigrants from Swinemunde, Germany, who purchased the brewery in 1882 and changed its name to the Upper Peninsula Brewing Company (UPBC).

The pair made structure improvements, replacing wood with brick and sandstone. On the forty-two-acre property at what is now called Meeske Street and US-41, Meeske built a bottling plant, warehouses, residences and a tower, which all resembled small castles. Along with Rublein's biergarten, these structures created a castle-on-the-Rhine atmosphere. By 1895, they were producing close to twenty-five thousand barrels per year at this location.

These buildings quickly became landmarks in Marquette. Meeske's home and office were located on the property and came with a tunnel that connected them to the brewery. The reason for this addition was perhaps one of the most interesting laws on the books at the time, which prohibited people from entering a brewery after sundown. With the tunnel, one could simply enter the brewery that way and avoid breaking the law.

One of the UPBC's most popular beers was called "Drei Kaiser," a name that lasted until World War I, when the name "Kaiser" became distasteful. The beer quickly changed names, becoming Castle Brew, and was sold throughout the UP. When Prohibition came, the company went out of business, and Meeske moved to Duluth.

The former Upper Peninsula Brewing Company as it looks today. *Photograph taken by the author.*

The castle-like structures, however, lived on. Some buildings were used to store goods for a trucking business; others housed a rock shop, law office and antique shop. But others were demolished to make room for a bank. In 1982, a local company called Humboldt Ridge restored Meeske's office to its historical specifications, and it lives on until this day.

ESCANABA

Escanaba flourished with the lumber and fishing industries. The first brewery in Escanaba was opened in 1874 by Shepley and Nolden, followed by the Joseph Nolden Brewery. A decade later, Henry Rahr, who hailed from a Green Bay brewing family, began building a brewery on the 1300 block of Lake Shore Drive on the site of an artesian spring. While the business was being constructed, locals drank Rahr beer from Green Bay or Schlitz from Milwaukee.

The Escanaba Brewing Company opened in 1887. Known for its Northern Beauty beer, like other breweries, it touted the purity of the product, stating that its beer was "mild, wholesome and nutritious…prepared under conditions of utmost cleanliness." As Prohibition loomed, Escanaba Brewing Company made Neerit, a "wholesome" cereal beverage, which was as essential a household product as needles. Despite this claim, the brewery closed during Prohibition.

John Richter, who had worked for Rahr in Green Bay, was the head brewer at Escanaba Brewing Company. He opened the second brewery in town, the Richter Brewing Company, in February 1901. Additions were made in later years, including a keg house, icehouse and bottling plant. The company sold its beer locally under the names Richter's Select and Richter's Special Beer. It touted its beer as having less than 4 percent alcohol, which gave it its "nutritive value" that also aided in digestion. Just before Prohibition, the stockholders changed the company's name to Richter Beverage Company and focused on selling nonalcoholic, non-fermented beverages.

By late 1918, the brewery had closed, and the beverage company was selling Ricto, a hoppy-flavored beverage made of cereal grain. The

The old Richter Brewery today. *Photograph taken by Dianna Higgs Stampfler.*

An old Delta Brewing Company crate on display at East Channel Brewing Company. *Photograph taken by the author.*

company pushed a local theme, encouraging residents to drink its beverage and keep money in the community. It sold enough soda—both its own and other nonalcoholic beverages—to become one of the few breweries to successfully pivot from beer to soft drinks.

After Prohibition's repeal, the company was reincorporated as the Delta Brewing Company. Its labels included Delta Lager Beer, Peninsula Pride, Buckingham Ale and Arctic Ale. This incarnation lasted until 1940. The building remained empty until the late 2000s, when the company was purchased to be renovated into loft apartments. The late Victorian–style building remains standing today.

MENOMINEE

Menominee, a lumber mill town located at the southern tip of the UP, on the Wisconsin border, welcomed early emigrants from Germany, Bohemia and Poland. With these newcomers came breweries, which began popping up in the early 1870s. These included the Louis Hartung Brewery, De Heck and Scharmbruch Brewery, Gauch and Berthold Brewery, Adam Gauch Brewery and the George Harter Brewery. One company began as Eichert and Skala Brewing in 1886, then became the Skala and W. Reindl Brewery in 1887 and ultimately became the Menominee River Brewing Company in 1888.

Leisen and Henes

John Deheck and George Scharmbruck opened a brewery in 1872; a year later, George Harter and Frank Eggard assumed operations. In 1876, John Henes and his father-in-law, Jacob Leisen, bought Harter's place and operated under the Leisen & Henes Brewing Company name.

John Henes was born in Gammertingen, Germany, in 1852. He came to America in 1871 and first lived in Wisconsin. There, he first worked in farming and later in brewing before landing in Menominee. Along the way, he married Rosa Leisen, and they had five children together. After serving as brewmaster for Adam Gauch, Henes launched a new venture with his father-in-law.

Leisen was born near Coblentz, Germany, and apprenticed as a cabinetmaker before serving in the Prussian army as a sharpshooter. After immigrating to the United States, he served in the Civil War before settling in Menominee.

A fire in 1877 and another in 1890 did not stop the successful brewery, even though the latter fire forced a complete rebuilding. In 1891, the Leisen and Henes Brewing Company incorporated and brewed on. In 1897, John patented the Henes-Keller bottling machine, which became the leading bottling machine in the industry. It featured a revolving filler and air pump, transferring beer from barrels to bottles without sacrificing any carbonation. As president of the Henes & Keller Company, John manufactured these machines, selling them globally; his son John E. Henes later patented an improvement to the machine.

In the late 1910s, realizing that state prohibition was coming, Leisen and Henes consolidated with the Menominee River Brewing Company, reorganizing under the name United Beverage Company. Using the Leisen and Henes plant, the company brewed "Near-Beer" (later called "Silver Cream") and sold soft drinks.

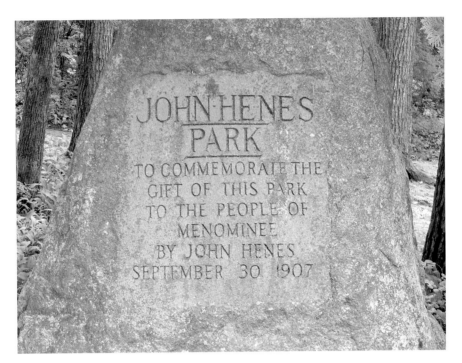

The stone commemorating Henes's land donation in Menominee. *Sourced from Wikimedia Commons.*

John Henes served as the director of the Lloyd Manufacturing Company (wooden goods) and as vice-president of the First National Bank, the Menominee River Sugar Company and the Richardson Shoe Company. He served as an alderman and supervisor of his ward and was on the board of Michigan's state prison and the board of trustees for Menominee's school of agriculture; he was also the president of the local German club and was an active Republican. In 1907, he donated land for a fifty-acre park that bears his name. Menominee's local newspaper said of him: "Mr. Henes is one of [our] most sterling citizens…[and] takes a place among the city's greatest benefactors. His name will be remembered with love and veneration." Henes passed away in 1923.

After Prohibition ended, the Menominee-Marinette Brewing Company opened in the old Leisen and Henes plant. It brewed for almost thirty years, introducing such labels as Menominee Bock, Big Mac Beer (introduced when the Mackinac Bridge was under construction) and a seasonal beer called Holiday Brew. It closed in 1961.

IRON MOUNTAIN

The Iron Mountain Brewing Company opened in 1891. Its closing date is unknown. The space became known as the Upper Michigan Brewing Company at some point before 1895 and ultimately produced 350 barrels of its Upper Michigan Lager Beer weekly. This incarnation lasted until 1899, when the Henze-Tollen Brewing Company was opened by owners Louis Henze and Gustave Tollen. Like many other breweries, the Henze-Tollen Brewing Company boasted that its beer was "pure without drugs or poison." By February 1920, after Prohibition began, Henze-Tollen consolidated with the Arbutus Beverage Company to sell cereal beverages and other drinks, such as root beer and grape juice. This business lasted until 1933. The Upper Michigan Brewing Company reopened after Prohibition was repealed, but this incarnation lasted only five years.

WESTERN UP

In the western corner of the UP is the Gogebic Iron Range, the last of the area iron ranges developed in 1880s. Like other new towns in this period, it soon found itself with many workers and breweries to satisfy them. Lumber, limestone quarrying, charcoal iron, a leather tannery and a pulp/paper mill industry all had about one thousand workers.

The John Held Brewery opened in in 1889 and lasted for four years. The Becker and Knapstein Brewery was open from 1898 to 1900 and was later renamed the Bessemer Brewing Company, which lasted until Prohibition. The Superior Brewing Company opened in 1901, became the Ironwood Brewing Company in 1902 and also lasted until Prohibition.

Willebrand-Manistique Brewery

In 1901, Theodore Willebrand opened the Willebrand-Manistique Brewery in a building constructed by his family. Alongside his sons and employees, Willebrand made beer that he kept cold with ice cut from Indian Lake. A tap and cup stood outside the brewery in case someone was walking by and felt like having a drink. Humans were not the only ones who enjoyed the beer—a fence had to be put up, as deer liked to drink the beer from drip trays, resulting in drunk deer wandering around.

Five years after opening the brewery, the Willebrand family sold their interests, and the place became known as the Manistique Brewery. Among its offerings was the popular Manistique Famous Beer. In 1909, John Brush and another arsonist set fire to the brewery, destroying hundreds of bushels of malt, hundreds of pounds of yeast and 650 barrels of beer. The brewery was only insured for $10,000, and it was never rebuilt.

2

WESTERN MICHIGAN

Nestled along the mighty Lake Michigan, the western part of the state boasts lighthouses, dunes, boats, rich culture heritages, beaches—and beer.

GRAND RAPIDS

Today, Grand Rapids is known as "Beer City"—a well-earned title for a city that boasts dozens of breweries and brewpubs. It also hosts the Michigan Brewers' Guild Winter Beer Festival, which is held annually in February.

Beer brewing and drinking started early in Beer City. In 1836, John Pannell settled at the bottom of Prospect Hill (now near Ottawa and Lyon Streets) and set up a small brewery. The Englishman made a "hop beer" for the town with fewer than one thousand residents, most of whom chose to drink whiskey. At first, Pannell brewed just a barrel per batch, but better days were coming.

Christoph Kusterer from Wurttenberg, Germany, first came to Ann Arbor and worked for A. Kern and his brewery. He then lit out for Grand Rapids. He joined Pannell, and the two collaborated for several years, brewing greater amounts of ale. They likely brewed English ales that were still hopped, but they also likely had a cleaner taste, thanks to Kusterer's German training.

Pannell heard the call of gold from the west and sold his shares to his partner in 1849. (He did not strike it rich and returned to western Michigan to farm before passing away in 1891.) Kusterer renamed the place City Brewery and moved the operation to the corner of East Bridge and Ionia Streets. The nearby spring, formerly a place where Natives frequently gathered, produced 40 gallons of water per minute, enough to brew 21 million gallons of beer every year, if one so chose. (No one chose to brew this much, however.)

Kusterer brewed the first lager in the area, involving himself in all aspects of the business, including the delivery of his product. Like so many other early brewers, Kusterer did not limit himself to beer; he helped found the German Evangelical Lutheran Church of Immanuel, served as the grand marshal for local parades and involved himself in the Grand Rapids Rifles. But he was the town's sole beer brewer for a time. By 1879, the *Grand Rapids Times* wrote that "no business house…is more generally known, patronized" than Kusterer's brewery, which, by then, produced nine thousand barrels annually and shipped product to locations as far away as Ohio and Indiana.

Kusterer's life came to a sad end when he died aboard the steamer *Alpena* while traveling to Chicago across Lake Michigan. The *Alpena* sailed on October 15, 1880, which was reportedly a clear, lovely day. About eighty passengers, twenty-six crew members and ten carloads of apples were on the main deck as the vessel set off. Around 1:00 a.m., the barometric pressure dropped precipitously, and a gale swept across the lake. Other captains spotted the *Alpena* and reported that it was "laboring mightily" across the lake. It was next spotted lying on its side. Some reports say that the ship swamped and sank or drifted off course and sank. Within days, debris and bodies began washing up on the beaches of the west side of Michigan. The actual wreck, however, remains lost. It is thought to be located somewhere between Holland, Michigan, and Racine, Wisconsin.

As they did in other parts of Michigan, German immigrants began arriving in Grand Rapids in the mid-nineteenth century. Gustav, Christian and Gottlieb Christ landed in Grand Rapids in 1850. Gustav and Christian worked for Kusterer for a short time before taking their knowledge of German beer to their own parcel of land, on which they built a malt house, brewhouse and icehouse. The G.&C. Christ Brewery advertised that its beer was analyzed by "Dr. DeCamp [and] is a much purer article and considerably healthier than any other beer." Drinkers must have appreciated this extra-special endorsement because the brewery thrived until 1873, when a fire wiped it—and one hundred other buildings—out. With community support to the tune of $50,000, the brothers were able to rebuild. Unfortunately, the business was lost to foreclosure by the early 1890s.

Left: An 1875 photograph of Christoph Kusterer. *Courtesy of the Grand Rapids Public Museum.*

Below: Kusterer's brewing building. *Courtesy of the Grand Rapids Public Museum.*

The importance of ice in the early days should be noted. Before refrigeration, breweries (and other businesses) had to harvest ice from the river. This was often a dangerous job, as one had to have horses pull plow-like ice cutters across the frozen water. The ice then had to be dragged to the icehouse and cut by hand.

A man named Mr. Anderson died at the Michigan Brewery in 1871 after being crushed by a piece of ice that weighed several hundred pounds.

In 1856, Grand Rapids boasted a Bridge Street brewery called Michigan Brewery, which was started by Peter Weirich. He strategically located his operation on the west side, near furniture factories where Germans with a thirst for beer worked.

At its peak, Weirich had seventy barrels set up, refrigerated cellars and piped in water directly from his farm. Weirich ran his company until his death in 1886; his successors changed the company's name to Peter Weirich Brewing Company in his honor. His son-in-law, George C. Bratt, hired a former Stroh's employee to run the operation, and the space was turned into the Petersen Brewing Company in the early 1900s.

In 1863, George Brandt opened the Union Brewery at 87 South Division Avenue, so named in support and honor of the Union troops who fought in the Civil War. Brandt studied under Christoph Kusterer at City Brewery before striking out on his own. Eventually, his son George and two associates, Fred Mayer and Christopher Killinger, joined the operation. When Brandt married Elizabeth Fluher in 1863, she also joined as a proprietor. The team mostly brewed lagers, as well as a cream ale and a stock ale. The company was consolidated into the Grand Rapids Brewing Company in 1892, and Brandt came full circle, as he once again worked with the Kusterer family.

Also from Wurttemberg, the Frey brothers left their mark in early Grand Rapids beer history. On Coldbrook Stream's banks, Carl and Christian Frey founded the Frey Brothers' Coldbrook Brewery in 1871, so called for the road it sat on and the water it was nestled next to (between Division and Monroe Avenues). Three years later, their older brother Adam joined the operation that eventually expanded and brewed more than ten thousand barrels of beer, selling to locations as far away as northern Michigan. They

Left: George Brandt. *Courtesy of the Grand Rapids Public Museum.*

Right: An advertisement for Union Brewery. *Courtesy of Grand Rapids Public Museum.*

were part of the brewery consolidation that formed the Grand Rapids Brewing Company (GRBC).

National Brewery was helmed by Adolph Goetz, whose pedigree included stints brewing in Germany, France, New York City and Cincinnati, the latter of which was one of the largest beer towns at the time. Goetz came to Grand Rapids in 1874, worked for a time with Kusterer and then joined with Kossuth Tusch to open the Cincinnati Brewery at 208 Grandville Avenue (near where Founders is now). It bore this name because it advertised itself as being "equal to Cincinnati beer!" Although Goetz sold his interest to his partner's brother, the brewery forged on to the point where it brewed ten thousand barrels a year.

Like John Pannell, Goetz intended to move west and find gold, but like Pannell, he returned to Michigan, eventually landing back in Grand Rapids, where he again worked with Kusterer. Goetz opened a saloon and used his proceeds from that business to start the National Brewing Company (near the current Mitten Brewing Company). This was also one of the breweries that was consolidated to form GRBC.

National Brewing Company. *Courtesy of the Grand Rapids Public Museum.*

National Brewery workers around 1890. *Courtesy of the Grand Rapids Public Museum.*

The Tusch Brothers brewing facility. *Courtesy of the Grand Rapids Public Museum.*

Right: Paul Rathman, date unknown. *Courtesy of the Grand Rapids Public Museum.*

Below: Veit and Rathman brewery workers. *Courtesy of the Grand Rapids Public Museum.*

Opposite: Veit and Rathman's Brewing Company, exterior view. *Courtesy of the Grand Rapids Public Museum.*

Another brewery that joined the consolidation was Jacob Veit and Paul Rathman's Eagle Brewery, which was opened in 1876 to honor the centennial of America. Located on the northeast corner of Frist Street and Stocking Avenue, it was a two-story building that employed about a dozen or so men who brewed lagers for the German population.

Between the years of 1875 and 1876, some non-German brewers attempted to brew ales. Aldrich Smith and William Draper brewed on the corner of South Division Avenue and Oak Street, while David Stiven's brewery was located at Canal and Coldbrook. Neither venture lasted for more than a year, presumably because of the locals' thirst for lagers.

The Grand Rapids Brewing Company

On August 7, 1895, locals smashed a beer bottle at 5:00 p.m. as they laid a cornerstone for a large stone building that looked like a castle. Designed by Lewis Lehle, an architect from Chicago, the building held the Grand Rapids Brewing Company (GRBC), a consolidated company of six Grand Rapids breweries: Kusterer's City Brewery, Tusch Brothers'

An advertisement for the Grands Rapid Brewing Company. *Courtesy of the Grand Rapids Public Museum.*

Cincinnati Brewery, George W. Brandt and Company, Veit and Rathman's Eagle Brewery, Adolph Goetz's National Brewery and the Frey Brothers' Coldbrook Brewery.

This conglomeration was formed in response to the competition from outside breweries that were selling their products locally. Larger American brewery conglomerates were buying up smaller breweries to increase their input and foothold in the area. Around the same time, British syndicates were instigating price wars. Smaller brewing interests were getting squeezed out, and something had to be done.

Well before that beer bottle smashed, the brewers had already been working together. At the end of 1892, they consolidated their companies and began brewing at the largest and most advanced brewery available: the Kusterer Brewing Company. Charles Kusterer served as president,

An advertisement for the Grand Rapid Brewing Company. *Courtesy of the Grand Rapids Public Museum.*

An advertisement for Grand Rapid Brewing Company, showing its beautiful building. *Courtesy of the Grand Rapids Public Museum.*

Jacob Veit as vice-president, Frederick Tush as secretary and Christopher Kusterer as treasurer.

Plans for a new facility were made. With cement brought in from Germany and reinforced steel walls, this place was made for brewers. And brew they did—sixty unionized men (from the Brewers Workingmen's Union No. 10 and the Beer Bottlers and Bottle Wagon Drivers Local 254) brewed fifty thousand barrels a year. By the turn of the century, the company's Silver Foam brand was being shipped to states both near and far. Much credit was owed to the spring on which Kusterer had built his operation—cherished water that was eventually enclosed in a room that filtered air and light from it. In addition to the widely popular Silver Foam, the company also made bock beer, Pilsner, porter and an unfermented "malt tonic" called "Hops and Malt."

The company's property included a bottling plant, stables for horses that were well known throughout the city for their beer deliveries (and even won some ribbons at local fairs) and glass-enameled stock tubs. A later expansion included a building of apartments, an auditorium and storage areas.

The GRBC brewers were purists when it came to hops; they never used chemical substitutes and purchased stock directly from Washington, Oregon and Germany. The company made its own yeast from strains from Munich and Vienna. All of the company's quality was maintained by its own quality control laboratory.

By 1916, the GRBC was producing an incredible 610,000 barrels a year, more than any other western Michigan brewery (until Founders in the mid-2010s). The conglomerate owned twenty saloons at one point and even opened icehouses in Hillsdale, Muskegon and Cadillac.

During Prohibition, it ceased its beer brewing operations but retained control over the machinery and facilities. Calling itself the Grand Rapids Product Company, it made ethyl alcohol and a byproduct called Silver Foam. On April 27, 1918, it sold beer out of the factory, and after selling out, the president at the time, Adolph Kusterer, said, "We're through for good."

Other Grand Rapids breweries in the early 1900s included the Petersen Brewing Company at 296 Bridge Street (formerly Weirich's business and located in his old building, which, by then, had been sold to Julius R. Petersen and Jacob Wipfler), Valley City Brewery (started in 1903), Furniture City Brewing Company (started in 1905) at the corner of Ionia and Wealthy Streets and Grand Valley Brewing Company (started in 1907) in Ionia. But by the time of Prohibition, there remained only three breweries: GRBC, Petersen and Furniture City. To make it through, Petersen made Vita, a

Goebel Brewing Company making a local delivery. *Courtesy of the Kalamazoo Public Library, Local History Room.*

soft drink that tasted like beer. Furniture City made Nu-Bru, a nonalcoholic beer, and sold ice. Furniture City considered getting into the grocery and dry goods business, but apparently, these ventures were not successful.

Despite Kusterer's proclamation of GRBC being done for good, the company made near beer in an attempt to stay afloat. When the company's near beer did not sell incredibly well, it had to close and sell off some of its assets, including its copper—including the pipes, tubes, vats, et cetera. This led to difficulties in getting the brewing systems up and going after Prohibition was repealed.

In 1932, GRBC filed articles of incorporation, and in 1933, it merged with Furniture Brewing Company with the intent of making legal beer. The new company's officers had some familiar last names—G.A. Kusterer, Frank Veit, Frank Neuman, George Gruenbauer and William J. Putle. They did not settle at their former location; instead, they bought what had been a shingle company, intending to restart their brewing operation there.

The company resumed production when Frank D. McKay, a wealthy local businessman and party boss of the state's Republican Party, became its secretary-treasurer. By this time, McKay had bought Muskegon Brewing Company and allowed GRBC to begin making beer at that factory, which was then shipped to Grand Rapids. Unfortunately, the beer did not regain its popularity; the company brewed at the Muskegon location until Goebel Brewing Company bought the property.

Chicago's Peter Fox Brewing Company purchased GRBC's assets after acquiring those of the Michigan Brewing Company.

Michigan Brewing Company

Meanwhile, Walter J. Conlon purchased the old GRBC property in 1935 with the intent of brewing beer as the Michigan Brewing Company. Until then, the castle-like building (which was originally the site of Kusterer's brewery) had been used mostly as a warehouse, but Conlon had grand plans for the old place—he was going to brew 300,000 barrels of Old Michigan Beer, a Pilsener-style lager. Conlon paid close attention to the space; he had built-to-order equipment, a large cellar space, a copper brew kettle, a filtered air-cooling room and steel malt hoppers. Frank E. Weber, a third-generation brewer, served as head brewer. (Weber brewed in one of Chicago's largest breweries, then served at Muskegon Brewing and Bottling Company and, during Prohibition, made near beer in Missouri.)

Conlon's flagship beer was named Old Michigan and was sold in short, fat twelve-ounce "brownie" bottles. Old Michigan beer was available on draft, in twelve-ounce bottles and in metal kegs, the latter of which Michigan Brewing Company had exclusive rights to in that part of the state. Unfortunately, Michigan Brewing Company could not make its enterprise profitable, and by June 1940, its assets were liquidated, falling into the hands of Chicago's Peter Fox Brewing Company.

In 1940, the Peter Fox Brewing Company took control of Michigan Brewing Company, using the defunct operation to both brew and assist with beer distribution. Its signature beer was Silver Foam; it also brewed Fox Deluxe Beer in Grand Rapids from 1941 to 1951. The building, located on Michigan Street, was later bought by the city, and the police department parked its cars on the lower floors. In 1964, the ten-unit complex of the old brewery buildings faced the wrecking ball as part of urban renewal plans. But the old building stood up to the wrecking ball, causing it to bounce right off the side before it ultimately fell.

OTHER POST–PROHIBITION BREWING

Grand Rapids and Michigan Brewing Companies were not the only breweries that attempted to make a go of things after Prohibition ended. The Imperial Brewing Company, which eventually became known as Valley City Brewing Company, was started in 1933. It made Valley City

Beer and Lohman's Ace High beer until it closed in 1940. For a short time, the Great Lakes Brewing Company opened at the site of the former Petersen Brewery.

Unfortunately, these closures all meant one thing—the western part of the state was dry as far as brewing beer was concerned. Drinkers relied on the large conglomerates, consuming Budweiser, Pabst and Schlitz. Coors arrived in the mid-1980s, right around the time a man named Larry Bell began his work at the Kalamazoo Brewing Company.

MUSKEGON

Muskegon Brewing Company was one of the largest breweries of its time, analogous to Bell's Brewery today. The brewery was located on Michigan Avenue, ran from 1876 to 1957 and was founded by three men: Otto Meeske, his brother Gustav Meeske and Gottlieb Ninnemann (sometimes spelled Ninneman). Otto came to the United States in 1871, with his brother Gustav showing up a year later, arriving in Muskegon via Milwaukee. The brothers purchased a small brewery called Neumeister and later formed a partnership with Gottlieb Ninnemann. Ninnemann

An advertisement for Muskegon Brewing Company. *Courtesy of Greg Haehnle.*

had been in the country since 1854 and in town since 1877, involving himself in city council and other civic boards.

The company grew over time, adding its own power plant in 1905 and installing an ice plant in 1915. It made its own malt and brewed more than twenty thousand barrels a year at its peak. The company survived Prohibition, thanks to its ice division called Pure Ice Company and by bottling nonalcoholic soft drinks, such as Hires Root Beer and Orange Crush.

In 1935, Frank D. McKay purchased the property, brewing beer for Grand Rapids Brewing Company that was shipped back to that city for drinking. The company was contracted to brew beer for the U.S. Armed Forces, becoming one of the major suppliers of beer during World War II. (Giant brewers like Pabst, Anheuser-Busch and Schlitz made similar contracts, allowing them to capitalize on the brand loyalty of returning veterans.)

Goebel Brewing Company bought the plant after the war ended, brewing, among other things, Guinness Beer until 1957, when it closed. (Goebel was one of the only breweries in America that produced Guinness, and it did so in seven-ounce bottles).

HOLLAND

In Holland, J. Aling started a brewery in 1863, brewing up to one thousand barrels by 1869. Unfortunately, the company was destroyed two years later by the Great Holland Fire that devastated much of the town, ruining dozens of stores and hundreds of homes, as well as hotels, churches and newspaper offices.

After the fire, in 1873, C. Zeeb from Milwaukee opened a brewery known as Holland City Brewery on Tenth Street and Maple Avenue. Later that same year, he sold it to E.F. Sutton and J. Steiner but appeared to stay on as a brewer.

Sutton bought out his partner two years later, and while his exact annual production numbers are lost to history, he was able to expand the operation in 1877. At the time, Cincinnati was a big beer city, and Sutton boasted that his next brew would be equal to or better than that city's "celebrated…lager beer.…So light and palatable that hardly any intoxicating parts are left in it." Alas, it seems that his beer did not come to fruition, as two of his brewers, the previously mentioned Zeeb and Anton Seif, bought the Holland Brewery. Sutton went on to open a saloon.

Zeeb and Seif learned the brewing trade in Milwaukee and worked together for a time before Zeeb left. Seif opened and closed saloons during the 1880s, ultimately opening one next to his brewery in 1891. Seif expanded the brewery's holdings to include a brick building, a cellar room and a bottling works.

In the 1890s, the ownership of the brewery vacillated between Seif and George Schoenith. By 1904, Seif was again in control of the company and renamed the operation Holland City Brewery, Anton Seif and Sons. Its tagline in the 1910s was: "a beer without a peer." It was sold in one of the city's eleven saloons, which were mostly owned by local brewers.

The *Holland City News* once said that a highlight of the brewing season was harvesting ice from Black Lake. The paper described bobsleds and horses dragging the ice from the lake up to Tenth Street, where it was dragged up chutes and then slid down into a giant icehouse.

Holland, like so many other cities, saw battles between the wets and dries. Local temperance supporters convinced the city council to raise saloons' licensing fees in 1877; this may have led to a significant decrease in the number of saloons in the city over the next decade (sixteen to seven). Saloons were forced to close on July 4, 1881, one of their busiest days, and in 1890, the licensing fees for saloons went up to $250.

Citizens in Holland said no to saloons via the ballot box in 1908, 1910, 1913 and 1916. This led to the increased demand for bottled beer, which was often consumed in public. Local private drinking clubs also gained steam. The "dry" writing was on the wall, however. Seif converted his plant into a cheese factory and purchased Banner Creamer in 1917. Holland Brewing Company began making cheese after more than fifty years of making beer, but it did not survive the 1920s.

Zeeland was a town that did not have a brewer, but it had plenty of liquor available. Local newspaper articles from the *Holland City News* report that local liquor sellers were getting into trouble with law enforcement for selling to minors; they also documented the opening and closing of local saloons. At one point in 1887, the paper reported that there were no saloons in Zeeland or Saugatuck, although it seems a saloon opened in Zeeland later that year. In 1899, the town passed an ordinance requiring a special license to run a saloon, plus the requirement of a $1,000 bond. Even after that, a saloon had to agree to not "disturb the peace... hire musicians...[or] associate with women of ill repute." The city became officially dry in 1906.

> The Zeeland saloon is closed. It's license expired and as another will not be granted, Zeeland people will have to come to Holland or go to Grand Rapids or Saugatuck to slake their thirst. All this because the

A Zeeland newspaper clipping lamenting the closure of its saloon.

49

KALAMAZOO

People have been living in this lovely area for thousands of years. Sometime before the first millennium, the Hopewell tribes settled there and lived their lives. After about the eighth century, the Potawatomi moved onto the land and were there when the Europeans arrived. The first White settler who built a cabin in what is now Kalamazoo was named Titus Bronson. He platted the town and named it after himself. In 1836, the name was changed to Kalamazoo, which comes from a Potawatomi word. Part of the reason it was renamed was Bronson himself—he was fined for stealing a cherry tree in 1836 and later run out of town.

The earliest brewers were English, making mostly British-style ales. Germans began arriving in the area in 1850, and with them came German-style lagers. But alcohol drinking in the region preceded these arrivals. Recipes published in newspapers as early as 1838 instructed locals on how to make beer using water, molasses and yeast, suggesting to perhaps add some spruce oil or spruce twigs for extra flavor. If one did not have malt on hand, the shells of green peas would do, the recipes advised. If treacle (sugar) was handy, one could make "sugar beer" by adding water, yeast and hops. These recipes came with a note of caution, urging consumption within a week, as the brews would not last for "any length of time."

According to the Kalamazoo Public Library's archives, the actual location and ownership of the first brewery in town (circa 1837) is the subject of conjecture. There is speculation that the first distillers in the town, Frank March and Thomas Clark, might have been involved. It's possible that a local brewer named Jacob Harlan might have run the operation on the north side of town. Some have said that the first brewery was located on Olmstead Road; others say it was located on Kalamazoo Avenue. What is known is that in 1842, "strong beer" was being offered at the Cash Store on Main Street and by 1850, several professional brewers were known to be in Kalamazoo, including Benjamin Hall, Jason Russell, Jacob Harlan, James Holmes and John Hall.

Englishman John Hall was born around 1799 and arrived in the area by at least the early 1840s, when he advertised that he would pay cash for hops and was producing vinegar for sale. In 1846, the *Kalamazoo Gazette* referenced a "large brewery of Mr. Hall" that had just begun operations at what is now Oakland Drive and Michigan Avenue.

Another Mr. Hall (possibly the brother of John, but this is not confirmed), Benjamin, was also an early brewer. Like the other Mr. Hall, he was from England and born around the turn of the nineteenth century. Benjamin

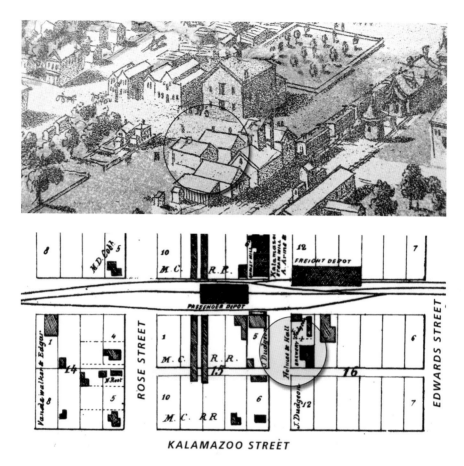

Top: A hand-drawn map of the location of Harlan's Brewery. *Courtesy of the Kalamazoo Public Library, Local History Room.*

Bottom: An early map showing the location of Hall and Holmes. *Courtesy of the Kalamazoo Public Library, Local History Room.*

partnered with Jason Russell and took over John Hall's brewery in May 1849. Within a year, they were brewing over fourteen thousand gallons annually. Despite this success, the business went up for sale in 1852.

Harlan and Holmes operated a small brewery on the north side of the town, on the east side of Burdick Street. Jacob Harlan left the trade in 1853, and James Holmes joined Benjamin Hall to open a saloon next door to the brewery on Burdick Street. After Hall passed away, Holmes continued to operate the brewery and saloon, producing about 11,000 gallons (350 barrels) a year until he died in 1863.

51

City Bottling Works, date unknown. *Courtesy of the Kalamazoo Public Library, Local History Room.*

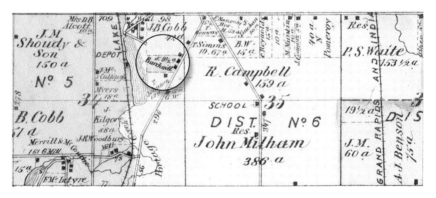

An early map showing the location of the Burchnall Brewery, circa 1873. *Courtesy of the Kalamazoo Public Library, Local History Room.*

In 1856, only two breweries existed in Kalamazoo. Fortunately, that changed quickly, as the number had tripled by the end of the Civil War. In 1852, John Williams advertised his "Small Beer" (the low alcohol by volume that was accepted by the temperance movement and enjoyed by day laborers) operation opposite the courthouse. His specialties included soda water, lemon soda and "Dr. Cronks compound Sarsaparilla Beer."

John Williams's operation was taken over by Myron Seymour, who made lemon pop and root beer. The business moved a block north and became known as the City Bottling Works, J.W. Rose being the proprietor. A local root beer maker took over the business in 1876. Henry Schoenheit, a partner in a mineral water bottling works, purchased City Bottling Works after the mineral water business ended. He built a new building on Portage Street and expanded to sell glass barware along with a variety of carbonated waters, lemon sour, cream ale, birch beer and often soft drinks. His homemade ginger ale was popular among the locals.

Dorothy and Joe Burchnall, English immigrants, landed in Kalamazoo in 1858 and opened a brewery on their family farm just three years later.

Joseph and Dorothy Burchnall, circa 1865. *From the collection of the Kalamazoo Valley Museum.*

Joe and Dorothy's daughter Mary Elizabeth married Thomas Westnedge. Their son was Colonel Joseph Burchnall Westnedge, a local celebrity. At the age of twenty-two, Joseph joined the Michigan National Guard. He then attended Kalamazoo College and led the football team to an undefeated 1895 season as halfback. He served as a captain in the Spanish-American War in 1898 and as a lieutenant colonel in the Jackson Prison Riots of 1911; he was promoted to colonel after serving along the Mexican border in 1916. During World War I, he commanded the 126th Infantry, part of the famous 32nd Red Arrow Division. Joseph proved to be popular with his troops, and he led them through many key offensives during the summer and fall of 1918. After the armistice, Joseph landed in an army hospital in France and died eighteen days after the war ended from complications of tonsillitis. His body was returned to Kalamazoo two years later to widespread mourning for "Colonel Joe." Thousands of people lined the streets during the funeral procession, and West Street was renamed Westnedge Avenue in his honor.

By 1865, the company was known as Old Joe's Brewery and was the second-largest producer in Kalamazoo, averaging sixty-plus barrels per month. It sold Burchnall's "Home Brewed Ale," nicknamed Old Joe's XX around the area and at local stores. Dorothy became the superintendent of the business by 1867 and continued operating the brewery after Joe's death in 1873.

Dorothy remarried after her husband's death, and the couple operated the brewery until 1878. Although beer and, later, malt liquors were made, Dorothy's ginger ale was the specialty of the house. The couple remained in the area to farm, but it appears that the brewery ceased operations. Dorothy lived until 1892, the same year that the brewery barn and house burned down.

OTHER KALAMAZOO BREWERIES

George Judge ran a successful malt house at 82 North Street in a former distillery. He mostly sold malted barley, rye and hops, but he was also known to brew amber and dark ales. In addition to supplying local brewers, Judge also sent malt to Goebel Brewing Company in Detroit.

Richard Frank started a brewery on the south side of what is now Michigan Avenue. He averaged about ten to thirty barrels a month, brewing until his death in 1865. The operation was then taken over by Henry Schroder, who married Frank's widow, Caroline. Henry Schroder was described as a "lively fellow" who enjoyed marching in local parades with his decorated beer wagon. He was also known for selling beer on Sunday and often made the acquaintance of the local judges because of it. With his taxes unpaid, revenue officers paid a visit, and according to the *Kalamazoo Gazette*, they "breached the barrels and sent their contents into the ditch." Caroline's son Albert Frank bought the property in 1884. The site was later purchased by a railway company, and the brewery was torn down to make way for an interurban line.

Slater's Brewery was located south of McKain's Corners in rural southeast Kalamazoo County, near what was a village of Scotts known as Pavilion. Slater served in the Civil War and operated a dance hall that he furnished with his homebrew. Slater lost a leg in 1880 and stopped brewing. He lived until 1885 and was buried in McKain Cemetery. (The village of Pavilion saw good times thanks to the railroad stops; after the railroad line was sold in 1910, the village disappeared and is now a ghost town).

A sketch showing the approximate location of the Frank Brewery. *Courtesy of the Kalamazoo Public Library, Local History Room.*

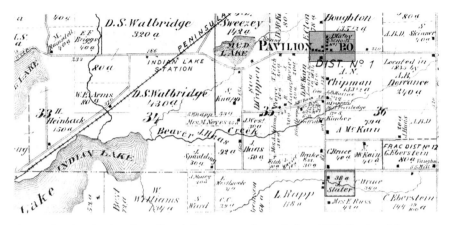

A map showing the site where Slater's Brewery was located, circa 1873. *Courtesy of the Kalamazoo Public Library, Local History Room.*

Portage Brewery was located in a small neighborhood near the outskirts of town on Winsted Street. Nicholas Baumann built it in 1856 and managed it for about three or four years. Baumann, who would turn out to be a major figure in the history of Kalamazoo and its beer, was born in Germany in 1828 and came to New York at the age of twenty-one. By 1855, he had traveled through the Allegheny Mountains to Kalamazoo. He worked for a local boardinghouse and then took the plunge into brewery life with his small business called the Portage Brewery.

After a few years, Baumann turned the brewery over to Gustav Sesemann, who operated the brewery to success, producing 850 barrels a year within his first year. Sesemann returned to New York City at the end of 1862, and William Hughes and Samuel True took over the brewery, calling it Burr Oak Brewery. True left, but Hughes carried on until 1870, when Fred Seyfferth took over. He ran it with his son Charles until about 1873. The brewery does not appear on liquor tax assessments past the mid-1870s, so it was presumably defunct by that time.

Kalamazoo Brewing Company

A political refugee from Germany named Lorenz Brentano operated a second brewery called the Kalamazoo Brewing Company. Built in 1857 along Walnut Street, the brewery lasted until 1879.

By 1858, Brentano advertised his "celebrated Bavarian lager beer and ale," offering free delivery. Brentano came to town with an impressive

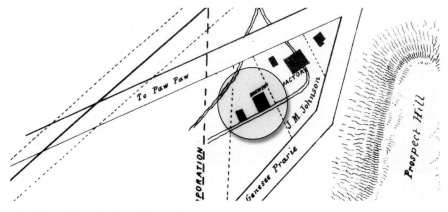

Above: An early map showing the Kalamazoo Brewery location, circa the late 1850s. *Courtesy of the Kalamazoo Public Library, Local History Room.*

Left: Lorenz Brentano, circa 1878. *Sourced from Wikimedia Commons.*

résumé. Prior to coming to America, Brentano studied law and practiced before Baden's Supreme Court, becoming widely known for his logic and argumentation skills. A leader of Baden's democratic left party, Brentano openly criticized the moderate government. He supported and participated in the 1848 revolution against the conservative aristocracy and was even elected president of the provisional republic. Ultimately, the revolution failed, and to avoid prison, Brentano fled to Switzerland. He came to the Pennsylvania in 1849, becoming a journalist and publisher of the antislavery journal *Der Leuchtturm*. After a year in Pennsylvania, Brentano landed in Kalamazoo County, where he farmed and brewed, living a "quiet life," according to the *Detroit Free Press*. After operating the brewery for a year, Brentano turned it over to the aforementioned Nicholas Baumann. He then

Top: A sketch showing Locher's Brewery, date unknown. *Courtesy of the Kalamazoo Public Library, Local History Room.*

Bottom: An advertisement for Locher's Kalamazoo Brewery from the 1867–68 city directory. *Courtesy of the Kalamazoo Public Library, Local History Room.*

relocated to Chicago with intentions to practice law and begin publishing again. Not only did he succeed in law, but he was also elected to Congress, ultimately becoming a top politician.

After a brief time, Baumann let Peter Herboldsheimer take ownership of the brewery. Relations between Baumann and Herboldsheimer turned sour at some point, leading to an argument that ended in the latter dumping a bucketful of hot beer over the former. Baumann suffered severe burns, and Herboldsheimer was tried, found guilty and served forty days in jail before leaving town, ultimately ending up in Kansas, where he passed away in 1862.

Bernhard "Barney" Locher took over the Kalamazoo Brewing Company on Walnut Street in the fall of 1862, selling harvest ale at nine dollars a barrel. Locher brewed alongside Albert Fogt and Michael Henkee, eventually running the second-largest brewery in the village by 1865.

Locher became an active member of his community. In addition to raising eight children with his wife, Theressa, he was the treasurer of the German Workingmen's Benevolent Association, a fireman, the treasurer of a local firehouse and a member of the German Harmonia Society. All the while, Locher grew his business, ultimately growing it to be the largest local brewery in 1874 with fifteen thousand barrels made each year. His bock beer sold well, but competition continued to grow, and that, along with a fire, led to a defaulted mortgage and the brewery going up for auction in 1879.

Nevertheless, Locher pressed on, opening a wholesale and retail ale house and bottling plant. Unfortunately, he suffered from health problems, including tuberculosis, and passed away just shy of his forty-second birthday. His wife operated the brewery for a while before the land was sold off and used for residential housing.

Kalamazoo Spring Brewery

Kalamazoo Spring Brewery stood along Arcadia Creek on Asylum Road. It was originally established by John Hall in 1847 and put up for sale in 1852. Sebastian Syke took over Hall's Kalamazoo Brewery in 1856 and soon went into business with a French master brewer, George Foegele (also spelled Foegle and Voegel). Their brewers included Fred Seyfferth and John Stearn.

In 1860, the brewery turned out the first German-style lagers in the area. It touted its beer as being useful for people "suffering from debility, ague and chill fever." This advertisement must have worked, as the brewery was soon selling about 1,500 barrels a year.

Syke later became a hotel keeper and liquor dealer in 1862, eventually becoming a farmer on what is now Michigan Avenue. Earlier in life, Syke fought against Napoleon, suffering injuries in the Battle of Leipzig. He lived a long life, passing away at the age of ninety in 1884.

After Syke left, Foegele joined up with Nicholas Baumann, who had been laid up due to his altercation with Herboldsheimer. By 1865, Foegele and Baumann were the largest producers of the four licensed brewers in town.

The brewery burned down in 1867 and was declared a total loss. Foegele left after the fire and became a local fireman and saloonkeeper. He became so loved that when he passed away in 1874, the local papers reported that the entire town mourned. Businesses closed for the day, and more than fifty carriages followed behind the three fire companies and town band to Foegele's final resting spot in Riverside Cemetery.

Baumann, who, by then, had taken over the business, rebuilt the next year, adding an underground ice-chilled lagering center and renaming it the Kalamazoo Steam Brewery after his brewing process. A relatively new process, steam brewing used a strain of lager yeast that fermented at higher temperatures, resulting in a lighter and cheaper beer that proved to be popular with working folks.

In 1871, Baumann sold his interest for what would be close to $1 million in today's currency and became a local developer, building the Baumann block on Burdick Street, as well as several stores, a saloon, a restaurant and a billiards hall. In addition to owning property and brewing, Baumann also dabbled in inventions. He received a patent in May 1869 for his "Improved Process of Using Unmashed Indian Corn in Brewing Beer." It is not clear if he used this method of brewing with maize in his operations at the steam brewery.

Baumann's sons became prominent local saloonkeepers, advertising that they were the first in town to offer the beer brewed by Anheuser-Busch. Baumann passed in 1895 at the age of sixty-seven.

After Baumann left, Charles Minard leased the space on Arcadia Creek. Minard was well known in the Detroit area for producing high-quality present-use (also known as "cream") ale; stock (or aged) ale; what he called "X, XX and XXX" ales; and porters. He dubbed his new venture Kalamazoo Steam Brewery and Malt House.

After Minard, Leo Kinast took over the business on Asylum Road, partnering with George Neumaier, who stayed until 1878. Kinast, in the meantime, carried on until his death from tuberculosis in 1881. After his death, attempts to revive the brewery were made but failed, and the building remained empty for years. A passing train sparked a fire in 1886, ruining the brewery. This event was celebrated by the local folks in the temperance movement as an "act of providence" to get rid of the "nefarious business of brewing the devil's drink" (this was said despite the fact that the building was empty). The remains were torn down in 1890.

Cold Stream Brewery

As was previously mentioned, Baden native George Neumaier began working at the steam brewery in 1872 and left in 1878 to start his own brewery. When Neumaier left, he took over the remains of the Taylor Thackwray on Lake Street and called his business the Cold Stream

Brewery. He retired in 1894, turning the brewery over to his son Alfred Neumaier, known as Fred, who had worked at Finlay Brewing in Toledo. Partnering with Leo Wagenman (also spelled Wagemann), the two formed Kalamazoo Union Brewing Company. They were so successful that Wagenman decided it was just too small for "his" business (as quoted in the *Kalamazoo Telegraph*). From newspaper reports, it appears that Wagenman intended to move the operation to a new and larger place, but his partner did not support this.

Nevertheless, in 1895, Wagenman bought a factory at Vine and Mill Streets, intending to begin his larger operations still under the name Kalamazoo Union Brewery. But in 1896, Fred Neumaier announced that he and Wagenman had parted ways and that he was moving to the building on Lake Street (the former Taylor Thackwray) to operate what he would call the City Union Brewery. In the meantime, Wagenman went ahead and brewed, releasing his Kalamazoo Union Beer at the beginning of 1896. Thus began something of a battle for drinkers—but it was really over before it began. Neumaier was a member of a well-respected family. His brewer father was involved with the local German Workingmen's Benevolent Association for years. The story was told that when an electrical worker became disabled, George bought an empty lot and built a grocery store there so the worker could run it while he recovered. This sort of loyalty carried over to Neumaier's new venture.

Wagenman, in the meantime, announced that he was selling his beer at a lower than "regular price"; despite this, local saloon owners and shops boycotted his brand and bought Neumaier's instead. By November 1896, Wagenman could not pay his taxes, so 465 barrels of beer were "turned out of the barrels and ran down Portage Creek, into the Kalamazoo River," according to the *Kalamazoo Gazette*.

Wagenman returned to Toledo shortly thereafter. Meanwhile, Neumaier kept improving his facility and was able to double his production by the turn of the twentieth century.

In 1904, City Union Brewery converted into a new stock company called the Kalamazoo Brewing Company, with Fred as the general manager. Increased pressure from larger breweries, plus the growing voices of the temperance movement/prohibitionists led the brewery to tout its beer as a healthful drink, much preferable to hard liquor. It pointed out that drinkers knew what was in its beer, as it was made locally and not subject to possible contamination or cheap ingredients like those from other areas. After the 1906 Food and Drug Act, the Kalamazoo Brewing Company stressed that its beer was made "pure and without drugs or poison," and it later advertised in

City Union Brewing. *Courtesy of the Kalamazoo Public Library, Local History Room.*

the *Kalamazoo Telegraph* that its beer was "highly recommended by physicians for its purity and quality."

Kalamazoo went dry in 1915. The only remaining brewery in the county was Kalamazoo Brewing Company, which had to halt production on May 1, 1915. The brewery equipment was sold off, and Fred retired. In 1917, the stockholders voted to sell and liquidate the property. The Kalamazoo Creamery Company bought the property and began operating as a pasteurization plant in 1919; it remained in business there until 1997. The building itself remained standing until 2011.

The last of Kalamazoo's original brewers, Fred Neumaier, passed away at the age of sixty-four in January 1937. He was buried in Riverside Cemetery.

LUDINGTON

Born in Wurttemberg, Germany, in 1845, Albert Vogel came to the United States and worked in Pennsylvania as a brewery foreman. After a brief stay in Chicago, Vogel moved to Pentwater and, again, took up brewing. Vogel

Delivering Vogel's beer. *Sourced from Find a Grave.*

arrived in Ludington in the 1870s and eventually bought twenty-five acres, where he built his brewery. To sell the beer he brewed, Vogel purchased additional land and constructed a beer garden and park, which was reported to have flower gardens and an aviary with pheasants, guinea fowl and peacocks. He closed shop in the early 1880s and worked as a distributor for Blatz and Best's of Milwaukee.

In the mid-1880s, Vogel bought property and got into the lumber business, harvesting hardwood trees. By 1893, he had his own sawmill that he used. Later, Vogel bought timber land holdings in Wisconsin, eventually becoming known as the "hardwood king." At the turn of the century, there was some speculation from local newspapers that there might be gold and copper on Vogel's lands; alas, nothing ever turned up.

Vogel married a woman named Sophia and had six children with her. He was a member of nine fraternal organizations and enjoyed high esteem in his adopted hometown. Vogel passed away from chronic nephritis in 1913 in Ludington.

MANISTEE

According to the *Manistee News Advocate*, the first brewery in town was built at the west end of River Street in the 1860s. But the largest, most modern brewery was built in 1884. Charles Daniels arrived in Manistee via Muskegon that year and constructed his brewery, which was considered extremely modern by that day's standards, at 14 Mason Street. The local directory listed that the brewery belonged to Charles Daniels and Joseph Gambs, but it eventually became known as the Manistee Brewing Company after Gambs left the business.

Daniels was born in Rostock, Germany, in 1830. He came to America at the age of eighteen, working his way from New York to Muskegon. He worked in sawmills and lumber camps and eventually worked as a driver for the Muskegon Brewing Company. Daniels married, had seven kids and bought real estate in his adopted hometown.

Daniels advertised that his drink was healthy and essential, mostly to avoid obstruction from the local temperance movement. To prove his point, Daniels asked prohibitionists to inspect the brewery, including a physician, who agreed that beer was wholesome and appropriate for patients suffering with various ailments. Daniels died from necrosis of the liver in 1906. His eldest son carried on the business under the name Charles H. Daniels Brewery, as it had been changed around 1911, operating until Prohibition. It attempted to make it through by brewing near beer but was not successful.

After Prohibition's repeal, the Gessell Brewery was listed in the city's directory, but it only appeared to last for a year. It was quite a year—an order for $250,000 worth of beer was received in 1933. A California distributor made the request that the local newspaper the *Manistee News* said "provided the most optimistic business news Manistee has heard in years," and it established the town "as one of the important business centers of the Middle-West."

Another Manistee Brewery Company operated for three years before being renamed the Chippewa Brewing Company. The Chippewa Brewing Company also operated from 1937 until at least 1948. (A Waldorf Brewing Company was also listed in 1935).

While mentions of Manistee beers are not common, one collector in Montgomery, Alabama, boasted that they had a painted glass sign advertising that Chippewa Beer contained "no glucose, no sugar, non-fattening." There is no word on how this early "light beer" might have tasted.

TRAVERSE CITY

Joseph Gambs landed in Traverse City, and he operated the city's first commercial brewery. In 1901, he sent out cards inviting recipients (and "the ladies") to his business on East Front Street. The Traverse City Brewery on 719 East Front Street opened on Wednesday, September 18, 1901, and offered free beer all day after 8:00 a.m. The German immigrant's specialty beer was the "hop vine beer." A Detroit architecture firm designed his brewery, which had an ice plant and boiler/engine room added in 1906.

In 1908, the Sleder brothers invested in the brewery and sold the beer in their saloon located on Randolph Street. Traverse City Brewing Company remained in business until Prohibition.

Note: The Sleder's Family Tavern, established in 1882, is known as the state's oldest continuously operating restaurant.

The interior of Gambs Brewery, which later became Traverse City Brewing Company. *Courtesy of the Traverse Area District Library.*

The Traverse City Brewing Company, 719 East Front Street, just before its demolition in 2000 to make way for the Hagerty Center. *Courtesy of the Traverse Area District Library.*

Breaking up the ice near the brewery. *Courtesy of Greg Haehnle.*

BATTLE CREEK

The first alcoholic beverage brewed in Battle Creek was whiskey; locally brewed beer did not arrive until John Stahl made it in 1858. Originally from Germany, Stahl built his first brewery on State Street and later moved to the hillside at Cliff and Elm Streets. Local German clubs and Irish clubs met at his brewery, where music flowed along with the drinks. In addition to his work as a brewer, Stahl was known for his expert marksmanship, winning awards in Michigan and beyond. Christian Martin, who later worked for the Western Brewery of Ann Arbor, spent three and a half years with Stahl. At that time, it seems the brewery was called the City Brewery; other records indicate that the name was simply the John Stahl Brewery.

In November 1900, the Battle Creek Brewing Company bought six lots at McCamly and Hamblin Avenues. The *Battle Creek Moon* described the future facility as an "architectural dream." It opened in 1901 and advertised in the *Morning Enquirer* that its beer was "the best of all—the sparkling pearl of bohemian export."

The brewery carried on until the county went dry in 1909, and it was forced out of business. The "local option" lasted for two years, but the issue of local prohibition did not go away. It came back up for a vote in 1913, leading to a heartfelt advertisement in the *Battle Creek Enquirer*. The brewery spoke of its two years under local option, when it sat idly by while Anheuser-Busch and Pabst beer shipments to the area increased. Another vote for a local option would mean "serious financial loss to its stockholders, many—and, in fact, most—of whom are mechanics and other working people of Battle Creek," it reasoned. Further, beer made outside of the city would be sent in large quantities "at the expense of a legitimate local industry," because "no one will pretend that no beer will be sent to Calhoun County" as the two years under the local option "fully [demonstrated] that the use of liquor in no degree diminished in so-called dry county." Those who were in favor of going dry again were "willing to destroy a local industry, owned by local men and women…confiscate its property…throw its employees out of work, merely to open up avenues of less competition to the rich and powerful breweries of Wisconsin and Milwaukee."

This argument must have worked, because the "drys" failed; however, Calhoun County voted to go dry again in 1915, closing the brewery for good. As of 1917, the directors of the company reorganized as the Battle Creek Ice and Cold Storage Company, which took over the space of the former brewery.

During the first local option, a legal question involving this brewery arose. In the case of *People v. Martin, 169 Michigan Reports*, it was reported that the Battle Creek Brewing Company reorganized in 1909 in Kalamazoo County and established an office there, which it was legally allowed to do in a "wet" county. However, it still retained its brewery and office in Battle Creek, even though it produced no beer there. A man named E.J. Mallory went to the brewery's office in Battle Creek and made an order for one case of beer from an agent of the brewery. The legal question that needed to be answered on appeal was whether the brewery had, by this action, made a sale of beer in "dry" Calhoun County. The court found that because an order was made and money was paid in the county operating under the local option, it was a sale that was in violation of the law. The brewery claimed that the order wasn't binding until it filed the order in its Kalamazoo office and had it approved by the secretary there, but alas, this argument was unsuccessful.

Post-Prohibition Battle Creek

After Prohibition, two breweries sprang up in Battle Creek: Food City and Silver Foam.

Food City Brewing, located at 200 Elm Street, stated in May 1933 that it would be the most modern brewery in the state and that it would be owned and operated by Battle Creek people; shares starting at one dollar each were advertised later that year. In 1934, the brewery could boast that its beer was the first to be brewed in glass-lined brew kettles and fermented in glass-lined tanks. It sold this beer until it closed in 1942.

Silver Foam was located at McCamly and Hamblin Streets at the site of the old Battle Creek Brewing Company, and it began its operations in 1933, producing lager beer in kegs while its bottled beer was brewed in Grand Rapids. Silver Foam lasted until 1939. Along the way, it won the exclusive rights to its trademarked name. The Grand Rapids Brewing Company had registered the name Silver Foam in 1892, but the company was dissolved when state prohibition took effect in 1918. After Prohibition's repeal, the

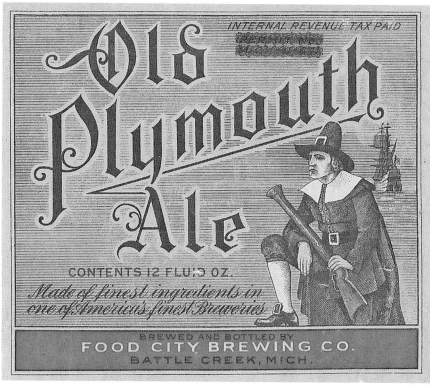

Above: Food City Brewing, Battle Creek Beer Label. *Courtesy of Stephen Johnson.*

Left: Silver Foam from Battle Creek, then owned and operated by Honer. *Courtesy of Greg Haehnle.*

Grand Rapids/Battle Creek Silver Foam Brewing Company incorporated, and in 1932, it registered its trademark. The Grand Rapids Brewing Company tried to get the name back, and the matter went to court. The Grand Rapids Circuit Court judge acknowledged the nostalgia of the name but ultimately ruled that there was no legal basis for it to be returned to the Grand Rapids Brewing Company.

BIG RAPIDS

Big Rapids boomed with lumber mills and worker camps in the late 1860s, and many times, the permanent population was equal to or surpassed by the number of workers in town; however, the strict logging camps did not allow drinking. The mills ran on a cycle of shutting down in March or April and then reopening in the fall, so during the springtime, the workers had time on their hands and money they had earned when the mills were operation. Some of that money could be spent at one of the three breweries in town.

Big Rapids' first brewery was located on Brewery Street off West Avenue. The brewery opened in 1868, the year that Big Rapids incorporated. It was operated by John Schlich, who also happened to be the brother-in-law of the man who owned Grand Rapids' Michigan Brewery. He and another in-law invested $1,000 and bought thirty acres of land. In 1871, the brewery was sold to Grand Rapids residents Robert Baumhoff and John Kurz. Baumhoff served in the Civil War and then worked for Christopher Kusterer along with Kurz. The two borrowed money to expand the space and brewed ales and lagers at the newly named City Brewery. Their "Sunday-Lager-Beer-Garden" event was reported by the *Big Rapids Magnet* as being a "regular hell" and likewise received grief from the local temperance groups. It is not clear if these events led directly to the local ordinances that disallowed liquor and beer sales on Sundays, but it is entirely possible that this was the case. At any rate, Kurz sold his part of the brewery to his partner, who carried on until financial problems forced the brewery into foreclosure in 1874.

In 1870, the Walker Brewery opened on Hutchinson Street. George and Sarah Walker and their three children came from England to Kent County in 1858. After the death of Sarah and George's remarriage, the family moved next to the steam mill in Big Rapids, where they brewed beer. After

P.A. Erikson and his brewery, circa 1883. *Courtesy of the Library of Congress.*

receiving money from a railway easement, the Walkers constructed a two-story brewery on the property, where ales and lagers were brewed for local saloons. George sold his brewery interests to his sons in 1872 and took up gardening. This was not a new venture for George, as he had previously been a gamekeeper and garden assistant for Queen Victoria.

George's sons continued brewing until each of them sold their shares and headed west. Albert Winter ultimately ran the operation before selling everything to a Grand Rapids banker, who rented out the brewery as a residence.

In 1878, Swedish-born P.A. Erikson and German-born Frederick Hoehn started a brewery on Swede Hill, across from the Europe House Hotel, which they also ran. Both owned saloons that sold their beer. Until 1892, the brewery was called the City Brewery, but it was later renamed Big Rapids Brewing Company. By 1901, the State Bureau of Labor had reported that the brewery was "idle," and seven years later, local maps showed that the brewery building and hotel no longer existed.

ELK RAPIDS

Elk Rapids is now home to Short's Brewery's Pull Barn Tap Room and Production Facility. Well over one hundred years ago, brothers Charles and Gottlieb Grammel opened Grammel's Brewery at 607 South Bayshore Drive.

By 1875, they were brewing a beer called "Silver Foam" and operating an icehouse on the Elk River. Charles operated under his own name from 1880 to 1888, and Gottlieb brewed under his own name from 1891 to 1895. At least two other breweries—Joseph Scurz's and John Berg's—operated briefly between 1888 and 1891.

3

MID-MICHIGAN AND EASTERN MICHIGAN

The upper lower peninsula and the middle of the state enjoyed many breweries from Germans, Englishmen and other immigrants. The area's fresh water and good soil led to many successful ventures.

JACKSON

Named after President Andrew Jackson and home to the first prison in the state, the city of Jackson enjoys a history that includes a crucial meeting of the early Republican Party and the birth of the Coney Island hot dog. It also boasts a brewing history that began around the mid-1850s, and by the time of Prohibition, it had grown to include over a dozen breweries, including the Jackson Brewing & Malting Company, Purney & Co., Adler's, the Haehnle Brewing Company and the Eberle Brewing Company.

Haehnle

The Haehnle Brewing Company was located on Lansing Avenue. Originally from Giengen, Germany, Casper Haehnle left his home country in 1854 came over to America alone. Before he left, he obtained a written agreement from his wife, Anna, that indicated she had consented to his decision to

An advertisement showing the Haehnle Brewing Company building. *Courtesy of Greg Haehnle.*

travel to America and that she had given him payments for these purposes. The understanding was that she and their children would follow along later. After sailing for about a month, Haehnle arrived in New York. For unknown reasons, his family never joined him; rather, his wife obtained a divorce from the royal court in Ellwangen, citing "criminal intention."

Haehnle moved ahead, marrying Amelia Baltz and settling in Jackson, where he started his brewery. Later, he opened another facility in Marshall.

During this time, his son from his first marriage to Anna arrived in America and lived with his father and stepmother. The elder Haehnle passed away in 1869, but fortunately, his son was ready to step in. At the age of sixteen, Casper "Cap" Jr. took over the businesses, focusing on the Jackson brewery, which he relocated to what became known as Haehnle Hill (and much later the I-94 interchange at North Cooper Street). Cap was brewing about five hundred barrels a year within the decade; in later years, at his peak, he produced about thirty-five thousand barrels a year.

In 1875, Cap married Mary Baltz, who was the daughter of his stepmother. His son Casper III and daughter Amelia were born soon thereafter. Cap was known as a kind, hardworking man who found work

Above: Cap Haehnle II and his family in the back of the original wood-structure brewery. *Courtesy of Greg Haehnle.*

Left: An advertisement for Haehnle's Fawn's Milk. *Courtesy of Greg Haehnle.*

for his men, even when there was really no need for it—because of this, his plant always ran at full capacity.

In either 1889 or 1891, a fire devastated the property. Because the brewery was beyond the reach of city water, it could not be saved. Unfortunately, the business was underinsured, but Cap announced his intentions to rebuild. He made good on these intentions, rebuilding a modern brewery at a great expense.

Two years later, in 1893, Cap passed away, but once again, there was a young son to step in. Casper III, then the same age that his father had been when he had taken over, took the reins in 1893, changed the company's name to Haehnle Brewing Company and brewed such brands as "Double Export" and "Fawn's Milk" (known as the "grand elixir for old stags"). Along the way, Casper III married Nelly Meyfarth and had one daughter, Phyllis. In 1901, he relocated to operate the Superior Brewery in Ironwood for about a year.

During Prohibition, Casper III sold tons of ice, which he harvested and stored at Devil's Lake; he also found time to establish the Windsor Wine Company in Walkerville, Ontario, Canada. In addition to these endeavors, Casper III also produced a "near beer" at the brewery (temporarily called

Haehnle Products Company) with 0.5 percent alcohol; this did not prove to be as popular as his real beer.

After the repeal of Prohibition, Casper III began making real beer again under the label "Old Hill Top," a nod to the location of the brewery at the highest elevation in Jackson. Casper III rented the brewery to Tucker North, who continued operations until 1937. Along the way, Casper III opened a brewery in Battle Creek called the Silver Foam Brewing Company. He later sold it to a relative named Bill Honer.

In his seventies, Casper III retired to spend time in nature, specifically at the estates he had purchased earlier in life. Much of his land was located along the Portage River, where he enjoyed hunting and fishing. He ultimately gave 497 acres of this land to the Michigan Audubon Society. The Phyllis Haehnle Memorial Sanctuary was named after Casper's only child, and thanks to gifts from Phyllis's daughter Judy Cory and additional purchases by the Audubon Society, the sanctuary now comprises over 900 acres.

Casper Haehnle III passed away in 1955 at the age of eighty-two.

Eberle

Carl Eberle came to Jackson from Bavaria in 1882 at the age of twenty-three. During the previous decade, he had been apprenticed to a brewer. He worked for Cap Haehnle at the Haehnle Brewing Company until he was twenty-seven, at which time, he branched out on his own, purchasing the Jackson Brewery at 901 Water Street. Within five years, he had replaced the old brewery with a four-story brick building.

The *Isabella County Enterprise* reported a fire at Eberle's brewery on May 12, 1891. The fire started on the roof and had spread to the rest of the building before the fire department could reach it. The plant was reportedly destroyed at a loss of $15,000, with insurance covering only $10,500; nevertheless, Eberle pressed on and rebuilt.

Eberle was said to be a "man of considerable public spirit." He served as president and treasurer of the brewery, with his wife, Sophie, serving as secretary and his eldest son, Carl F. Eberle, serving as vice-president and manager. His daughter Sophie, a graduate of the Jackson Business University, was the bookkeeper. The company was entirely family-owned.

Eberle brewed at least half a dozen beers under brand names like Club Ale, Jackson Beer and Blue Star Beer, the latter of which was shipped statewide and advertised as the beer "without a headache."

Eberle Brewing beer. *Courtesy of Stephen Johnson.*

Well before Prohibition, Eberle crafted seven soft drinks. When Prohibition became law, he changed the company's name to Eberle Beverage Company and pivoted to soft drinks, such as Sweet Sixteen, Frostie Root Beer and Imitation Orangeade. Eberle bottled the popular Delaware Punch, which is now owned by Coca-Cola and available in some parts of the South, but sadly, it stopped being sold in Jackson in 1964. The drink originated from a Texas inventor named Thomas Lyons. Its taste is described as "grapes drenched in sugar," and it's said to be the "color of Merlot wine."

After Carl died of a heart attack in 1927, his sons Erwin A. and Carl F. Eberle assumed control of the company's operations. They were at the helm when Prohibition ended, and they quickly brought back the Blue Star Beer at the rate of 243 barrels a day. A new bottling machine helped the company distribute its Blue Star Beer around the lower peninsula less a year later.

In 1941, the company's name was changed to Eberle Bottling Company, and it ceased brewing beer, lending all its attention to soft drinks. This decision proved wise, as the start of World War II saw national beer brands draining the market share from local breweries. The company remained in the family until it was sold in 1964. The new owners moved to a new location and closed the brewery's doors shortly thereafter.

On April 13, 1909, Jackson voted to go dry, with the "local option" law to take effect on May 1. The 1911 Michigan Supreme Court case of *People v. Eberle* (167 Mich. 477) indicated that in September 1909, the local sheriff and two deputies raided Eberle Brewing Company for possessing near beer, nearer beer and real beer. Warrants were issued to the officers of the brewing company for being in violation of the local option law, as they had manufactured beer after May 1. The defendants were found guilty, a ruling that was upheld on appeal. Notably, the vice-president, Stephen H. Carroll, had been the boss of common council for twenty years and a local leader of Democratic Party.

The case specifically discussed the Michigan local option law of 1889, which gave permission to local electorates to prohibit the manufacture or sale of intoxicants. Later amendments in 1899 and 1901 said that this law did not apply to wine or cider made from homegrown fruit in quantities smaller than five gallons and further allowed the sale and manufacture of wine and cider in dry counties. In other words, cider and wine made from homegrown fruit was exempt from the local option law.

In the context of this case, the Michigan Supreme Court held that the amendments permitting the manufacture and sale of wine and cider in dry counties to be an unlawful discrimination against the products and citizens of other states and that they were in violation of the equal protection act—making them invalid. However, the court upheld the guilty verdict of the defendants, reasoning that the original 1889 local option law was still valid and had not been rendered invalid just because the subsequent amendments had.

The case made it all the way to the United States Supreme Court (232 U.S. 700), which decided the case on March 23, 1914. Justice Lamar issued the opinion, which affirmed the Michigan Supreme Court's reasoning and ruling. He affirmed the rule of the law, stating that the validity of a local option law was not affected when the amendments were later found to be unconstitutional.

LANSING

Lansing Township was named Michigan's new capital in 1847. Early settlers were "horrified" that there "was not so much as a village at the location [in this] howling wilderness." Nevertheless, a wooden building was quickly erected there, and settlers began arriving. It was first called "Michigan, Michigan," which proved to be extremely confusing; the name was soon changed to Lansing. It became a city in 1859.

Other historians have noted that Lansing did not have a great number of brewers, relying instead on the breweries in Milwaukee, Chicago, Detroit and Grand Rapids to supply its share of beer. Nevertheless, some memorable local options for beer did exist.

Frederick and Anna Weinmann (also spelled Weimann or Weiman) and their baby arrived in Lansing from Warttenberg, Germany, sometime in the late 1840s or early 1850s; Frederick soon announced his intentions to be a commercial brewer. By 1856, he had a flourishing enterprise at the northeast corner of Maple and Pine Streets. It is known as the first of the half dozen breweries that would exist in Lansing and East Lansing between the mid-nineteenth century and Prohibition.

Weinmann's location proved to be ideal—it had a freshwater stream to provide water and creek banks that allowed a simple dig for a cooling center. Two buildings with long porches were erected, and they overlooked a beer garden that was placed in a stand of maple trees. A contemporary book described "lusty Germans…heard singing drinking songs late into the night." While Frederick brewed in the back, Anna served customers in the front. They also had a cabbage patch, pigs that fed on the waste malt and cows in the pasture.

The brewery became known for its amber cream beer, and the business flourished until around 1858, when new neighbors moved in directly west of the brewery—the Lansing Female Seminary. This select school, started by Abigail and Delia Rogers, attracted young women from all over the region. As it happened, the only driveway into the school led directly past the brewery. The school leaders objected to being forced to pass by the brewery and smell the growing hops, brewing grains, sauerkraut pickling and pigs fattening themselves on waste malt. The nightly singalongs around midnight, where patrons of the brewery delighted in singing "Watch on the Rhine" and other drinking songs of the day, also aggrieved the school's leaders. The Rogers sisters took up the matter directly with Weinmann, resulting in him agreeing to not to expand the beer garden on his property.

A. FOERSTER,
MANUFACTURER OF
LAGER BEER
ORDERS FOR
Kegs ₰ Bottled Lager
Will receive Prompt Attention.
GRAND RIVER BREWERY,
LANSING, MICH.

An advertisement from the 1883.
From the Lansing City Directory.

This decision led to diminished profits and ultimately contributed to the failure of the brewery.

The school was later known as the Michigan Female College, the Odd Fellows Institute and, ultimately, the Michigan School for the Blind. The Rogers sisters were part of first wave of the women's movement and the temperance movement.

The nineteenth-century city directories listed additional breweries in Lansing. George Schlotter owned the City Brewery on Jefferson Street, near Grand River. It was a small operation that was opened in 1865, and it was out of business by 1880. In 1865, Yeiter & Company started a brewery at Washington Avenue and Madison Street that lasted for about a year under that name. The brewery then became known as the Grand River Brewery. The *Lansing State Journal* reported that for "25 cents, a drinker could get six big schuper [glasses] of beer." Yeiter & Company carried on until it sold to Adam Foerster in 1880, who ran the brewery until it closed in 1884.

After moving from Ypsilanti to Lansing in 1874, Adam Foerster started his eponymous brewing company. Since the brewery was located near the Grand River, Foerster was able to harvest ice in the winter. The *Lansing State Journal* called the harvest a "big winter show"—horses, machinery and workers were all ready to go when the river froze over. Workers were given beer while they worked, kids slid on sleds and a good time was had by all—especially the following summer, when beer drinkers could enjoy their beverages on ice. According to the *History of Ingham and Eaton Counties of Michigan*, Foerster ran both his own brewery and the Grand River Brewery. The former also had a bottling house located near the railroad. By the 1890s, both places had gone out of business, allowing Lansing Brewing Company to expand further.

Lansing Brewing Company

The Lansing Brewing Company was the main beer maker in Lansing in the years before Prohibition. Located on the corner of Turner and Clinton Streets, it began its operations in 1898, not too long after Ransom Olds drove a gas-powered automobile down the city's streets.

The president and driving force of Lansing Brewing Company was Lawrence Price, who was born in County Tipperary, Ireland, on May 27, 1843. At the age of six, he sailed to America with his family, landing in Lewiston, New York. Price served in the Civil War in the Army of the Potomac, fighting at Antietam, Fredericksburg and, finally, Chancellorsville, where he was wounded by a shell. He recovered to fight at Gettysburg, where he suffered a wound to his arm. Despite this second wound, Price stayed on, joining one of the first batteries that entered Atlanta and then headed to the coast with Sherman. In late 1864, the troops traveled north, where Price suffered an injury to his face; he was later taken prisoner by the Rebels and sent to the Libby Prison. After Richmond surrendered, the Confederates released the Union prisoners, and Price found himself at a camp in Maryland. Although he was given a month-long furlough, he only took a week off before joining up with his regiment once again, ultimately ending up in Rochester, New York, at the war's end.

Price stopped in Lansing before setting out for Pennsylvania to work in the oil fields. In 1866, he returned to the Lansing area, where he worked on a farm and bought property in Bath Township. Price farmed and built multiple structures on his one hundred acres. He worked in the produce and grocery business before selling those interests and buying property in Lansing proper, where he became involved in the lumber business. He served as the vice-president and a director of the Capital Lumber Company, amassing wealth along the way.

Price launched many enterprises in Lansing, including the Lansing Brewing Company in 1898. While he was involved with the brewery, Price served as the president of Auto Body Works, and at one time, he had interests in and served on the board of numerous automobile companies—he was an original investor in the REO Motor Car Company. An active Democrat, Price served as a member of the city council, the superintendent of public works and the first chair of the Board of Supervisors. In 1890, he was appointed chief of police and marshal of the city of Lansing. Price was described as a man "endowed by nature with a vigorous mind, retentive memory and resistless determination." He passed in 1917.

Lansing Brewing Company's beer of choice was its Amber Cream Ale. Local temperance and Prohibition led to the brewery's closure in 1914.

Ingham County enacted a local ban on the sale of alcohol in 1910; it went wet again two years later before officially going dry in 1914, six years prior to Prohibition going into effect nationally. Lansing State Brewery was relicensed in 1933, but it never reopened, likely due to a lack of financing.

Price's widow, Julia, held the note to the home of Andrew Kehoe. Kehoe was a farmer who killed thirty-eight children and six adults and injured fifty-eight others when he detonated bombs at the Bath Consolidated School on May 18, 1927. Some reports said he was angry that he had lost reelection as treasurer of the school board. This "anger" led him to kill his wife, Nellie (born Nellie Price), and then commit the largest mass murder of school children in U.S. history. He died by suicide when he detonated dynamite in his truck—this explosion killed several other people who happened to be in the vicinity.

The *Lansing State Journal* published an article that gave a different cause for his "anger," writing that the "foreclosure of [the] mortgage on Kehoe's farm by [Julia Price]...is believed to have crazed the man and caused him to seek revenge on the community." Because of these statements, some locals held the rich widow partially responsible for the heinous crime. However, Grant Parker's book *Mayday* notes that these statements were, at best, unjust and possibly libelous.

BAY CITY

Brewing in Bay City began along the Saginaw River in 1865. John Rosa erected a brewery that was known as West Bay City Brewing Company in 1868 (there were reports that it had another recorded name, but it has been lost to the ages). Rosa and a fellow brewer named Andrew Fink began their operation making five thousand barrels a year.

Through the years, the brewery's ownership changed, but it carried on until a devastating 1896 fire. When it reopened, it had a new name—Phoenix Brewery, in honor of the fact that it had literally risen from the ashes. It also had new branding in the form of the eponymous bird rising from a flame and an added brewing capacity of twenty thousand barrels.

Louis Hine, a member of a longtime Bay City family, assumed the role of secretary-treasurer in 1897. In Moore's *History of Michigan*, he credited Hine's active role with helping the brewery become large enough to employ thirty "expert workmen" and to have a large "bottling and shipping business to all parts of the state." Hine also served as the vice-president of the Hine Lumber Company and as a director of the People's Savings Bank.

To survive Prohibition, the brewery began producing and selling malt extract for home brewers. The five-gallon cans were sold until 1933, when the company was reformed under the auspices of Hans Behrens, who had served as the company's head brewer from 1910 to 1918. Before and during World War II, Phoenix increased both its storage and production of its Phoenix Beer trade name, becoming known for its "cone top" beer cans. Unfortunately, it was unable to compete with the national brands that were muscling in all over the country. In 1952, the mighty bird that had risen from the ashes closed its doors for good.

Note: This John Rosa is a different John Rosa from the one who started Saginaw's Eagle Brewery; however, they may have been cousins. John's (Bay City) daughter Emelia married Frederick Kolb, who was the son of George Kolb, the founder of Salzburg Brewery, later named Kolb Brewing Company.

Kolb

Native German George Kolb founded Salzburg Brewery in 1867, when he was around forty years old. He spent most of his life in the beer business and passed away in 1892; he was buried in Oak Ridge Cemetery in Bay City.

After the passing of the founder, George Kolb II ran the brewery, which was located at 603 Germania Street and known as the Kolb Brewing Company after 1907. During Prohibition, it changed its name to Kolb Cereola Company Brewery and made Cer-ola, a non-intoxicating cereal beverage that was advertised as "a triumph in soft drinks." Kolb closed in 1939.

George's great-grandson Robert and his father started Kolb Sales-Distributors of Quality Beers after Robert returned from fighting in World War II. The company delivered the popular Buckeye Beer throughout eastern and central Michigan.

Bay City Brewing Company

According to Charles Moore's *History of Michigan*, Walter D. Young began working in the brewing business in 1877 under the firm name C.E. Young

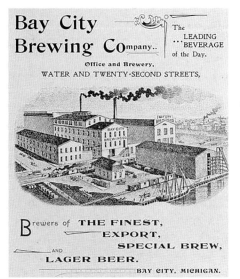

Left: A Bay City Brewing Company advertisement showing the building. *Courtesy of Stephen Johnson.*

Above: Bay City Brewing's "finest beer" label. *Courtesy of Stephen Johnson.*

& Company (but he changed the name to the Bay City Brewing Company in 1884). While Young stayed on as the president of the brewing company, he engaged in many other business ventures, including the Michigan Log Towing Company and the Young Transportation Company. He also served as the vice-president of the German American Sugar Company, vice-president of the Bay City Bank and a significant landowner in the Bay City area. Moore's book indicates that the Young was a "man of charitable impulses [who had] done much for the worthy poor."

Early advertisements for Bay City Brewing Company (a name that now belongs to a brewery in San Diego) claim the company made "the finest… special brew" lager. Its facility was located along the Saginaw River at Water and Twenty-Second Streets. Online records show that after Prohibition, the company reopened as Bay City Beverage Co. It closed its doors in 1943.

FRANKENMUTH

It is perhaps no surprise that the first brewer in Frankenmuth was from Bavaria; to this day, the area is known as "Little Bavaria." It is home to a thriving tourist industry and is fun for anyone who is looking to enjoy German hospitality and the area's famous chicken dinners.

John Matthias Falliers and his wife arrived in town and set up the Frankenmuth Brewery in 1857. It only had the ability to hold two hundred gallons, but at least the town of German immigrants had beer. John ran the brewery until 1864, and he passed away in 1866. This endeavor was known as the Frankenmuth Brewery (not to be confused with the current Frankenmuth Brewery).

There was also a Frankenmuth Brewing Company (not to be confused with the late 1980s Frankenmuth Brewing Company) that operated in the small town in the days before Prohibition. Frankenmuth Brewing Company began in 1899 with a meeting of potential shareholders, who brought with them handfuls of cash that they had squirreled away in their homes. John Adam List led the charge, and the brewery opened in 1900. Its capacity topped out at ten thousand barrels per year; patrons could purchase the brewery's product at their local tavern or in kegs to bottle at home. Of course, production had to come to an end in 1918, but six years into Prohibition, Otto Rosenbush purchased the plant to make malt extract. He reopened as the "Frankenmuth Products Company," which made malt and an alcohol-free beverage called Franko.

Once the Volstead Act (Prohibition) was repealed, the company went back to its original name and expanded to make an incredible 100,000 barrels

The original Frankenmuth Brewery, now the site of Frankenmuth River Place. *Courtesy of the Frankenmuth Chamber of Commerce.*

per year. The prosperous business was sold to Detroit investors in 1934; twenty-one years later, these investors sold out to a new corporation called International Breweries Inc. A year later, the brewery was sold to the Carling Brewery of Canada, which modernized the plant to produce 800,000 barrels a year while being known as the safest brewery in the country (operating thirteen years without an accident).

Unfortunately, Carling went from being the fastest-growing brewer to one of the fastest-declining brewers, and it was sold to G. Heileman Brewing of LaCrosse, Wisconsin. Heileman expanded the brewing facility in Frankenmuth in 1983, eventually brewing an unheard of (at the time) 1 million barrels per year.

The G. Heileman operation was acquired by Alan Bond in a leveraged buyout for $1.7 billion in 1987. As it turns out, Bond funded this purchase with junk bonds. When his financial empire collapsed, the G. Heileman Brewing Company declared bankruptcy. A private equity firm bought the company in 1994 and then sold it to the Stroh Brewing Company in 1996. When Stroh was split between Pabst and Miller, the G. Heileman brand and its intellectual property became part of Pabst, which continues to produce brands such as Old Style and Special Export.

Geyer Brothers

The Geyer Brothers' Boyne Falls beer label. *Courtesy of Stephen Johnson.*

This brewery exists today as the Frankenmuth Brewery; it is credited with being the oldest microbrewery in the state, as it was established in 1862.

Cousins William Knaust and Martin Heubush began the Cass River Brewery in 1862 two lots away from the property owned by Falliers. A dozen years later, they sold to John Geyer, who changed the name to Geyer Brothers Cass River Brewery and ran it with his sibling, J. Michael. They expanded in 1890, as Geyer had trained his sons, John L. and Fred, as brewers. The sons took over the company's operations in 1908, shortening the name to Geyer Brothers Brewery.

This brewery was one of the rare ones that survived Prohibition. John and Fred made malt extract, which was publicly advertised for use in breadmaking, but in practice, it was usually used in the homebrews of

The Geyer Brothers' property, now the site of the current Frankenmuth Brewery. *Courtesy of the Frankenmuth Chamber of Commerce.*

residents. After the Volstead Act was repealed, the company went back to making beer and was successful enough to expand.

John and Fred retired in 1949, and the third generation took over. By the 1960s, Geyer Brothers was the second-oldest small brewery in the state; only Stroh had a longer continuous history. It soldiered on against competition from the bigger brands, including Stroh, until 1986, when it closed up shop.

Two years later, Ferdinand "Fred" Schumacher and Ervin Industries bought the business out of bankruptcy and reopened the brewery as Frankenmuth Brewing Company Inc. In 1990, Randall Heine bought majority ownership.

Schumacher was born into a brewing family in Dusseldorf, Germany. His name, Brauerei Ferdinand Schumacher, was given to one male son per generation, indicating the intentions for him to run the family brewery. He would have been the fifth-generation brewer of the business, but World War II intervened, and the family brewpub was bombed in 1942. Fred worked as a brewery apprentice before taking a brewmaster's exam. He spent two years in Cologne brewing Kolsch beers. At the age of twenty-one, Schumacher headed to Australia to work at Foster's Brewery for two years. Eventually, he followed some advice from his grandfather to come to America. After working in nonbrewing industries, earning a high school diploma and attending college, Schumacher landed a job with Schlitz. The years he spent at this job provided him with the knowledge and experience he needed to open his own brewery—he just didn't have the money to do so.

Old Cass River Brewery. *Courtesy of the Frankenmuth Chamber of Commerce.*

He happened to be in Detroit in 1986, when a distributor suggested that he visit Frankenmuth. There, he saw the Geyer Brothers Brewing Company in disrepair and had an idea, but he learned that he would need $3 million to bring this idea to fruition. Since Stroh had closed its Detroit plant, Schumacher bought its barrel tanks on credit, found a brewmaster from Weihenstephan and had the leverage to get a financial backer. After a couple of misfires with brewmasters and recipes, he found a new brewmaster but lost investors. A local investor named Randy Heine showed interest but wanted sole control, which Schumacher eventually agreed to.

On June 21, 1996, Frankenmuth was hit by a tornado that destroyed four homes and damaged over one hundred others. Directly in the storm's path was the brewery, which sustained heavy damage and did not recover. The wrecking ball took down everything but the brew house on August 30, 1996. (An interesting fact: this author, her mother and her aunt had planned a trip to Frankenmuth that day but canceled because of the weather forecast.)

The current iteration of the Frankenmuth Brewery reopened at the site of the former Geyer Brothers Brewery in 2003.

Eagle Brewing Company at Fayette and Throop Streets. *Courtesy of the Saginaw Public Library Archives.*

SAGINAW

The first brewery in Saginaw opened in 1854. Located on the west side of town, the Eagle Brewery was operated by John Wolfgang Rosa, who came to the United States from Germany in 1845. After working in breweries in Detroit and Ann Arbor, he started his business at his home, but it soon grew into a full brewing company and bottling works. His sons trained as brewers and eventually took over the family business. The brewery stayed in the family until it was sold in 1914. Just two years later, a fire destroyed the building.

Schemm

In 1864, German immigrant John G. Schemm moved to Saginaw, and he began his brewing operation in the 900 block of North Hamilton two years later. Born in 1830, Schemm came to America when he was twenty-two. He settled in Detroit but relocated to Saginaw after his father's death. He brewed with Christian Grueler under the name Schemm & Grueler until

Grueler's death in 1869. He later brewed with a Mr. Schoenheit, but by 1874, Schemm operated alone. John Schemm passed away in 1899, and his son took over his business. Schemm's obituary said that he was "esteemed by all who knew him as a true man."

Known for brewing some of the best beer in the Saginaw Valley area, the brewery grew as the decades passed. It purchased the Star Brewery on Lapeer Street, expanding to produce seventy-five thousand barrels a year. It tried brewing nonalcoholic beer after Prohibition went into effect, but these drinks did not prove to be popular, and the property fell into the hands of the Bank of Saginaw. After Prohibition's repeal, the bank sold the property to Detroit investors headed by John Gillespie. The other investors were not identified, and a battle with the state liquor license board, which suspected Purple Gang involvement, ensued. When new owners took over the company in 1938, the state finally approved the liquor license, but the facility only operated for a year before the city took over for failure to pay property taxes.

National Brewing Company

The National Brewing Company in Saginaw was started by Peter Raquet in 1885. Peter and his brother Jacob initially began brewing together on Lapeer Street in 1870 under the name P.&J. Raquet; however, they split, and each began their own separate brewery.

Located at the corner of Genesee and Walnut Streets, the National Brewing Company focused on local labor, materials and drinkers. When Peter passed away in 1890, his sons-in-law took over the brewery's operations. After a buyout of one of them (J.L. Hubinger) and the death of another (George Wolfarth), a remaining son-in-law, William F. Weber, and Peter's daughter Emma Wolfarth ran the company (leasing the building from Peter's widow, who had inherited it). Weber was quoted in the December 9, 1897 edition of the *Saginaw Evening News* poetically touting his product, saying the drinking of lager "should be encouraged by the government; it is in the power of all to secure it by reason of its low price, and its cheapness assists in making it such a great moral agent. Lager beer, after a short acquaintance, becomes an associate, nourishing and sustaining to the purchaser. It possesses so little alcohol and such health-giving power that it can defy competition. Beer has been introduced by the most conservative families into their houses as a temperance drink. In my opinion, the phenomenal increase in the sale of malt liquors the past thirty years is the most powerful argument for beer as a popular and healthful beverage."

The business grew, taking over the city block with separate buildings. This was likely due to the laws that forbade the sale of beer at a brewery, requiring a separate building for sales and tasting. There were also rumors of tunnels between the buildings on the property; this was likely due to laws that prohibited one from entering a brewery after the sun set.

Brewing a nonalcoholic drink called Nabo and bottling soda pop kept the brewery afloat during Prohibition. It made beer again in 1933 and switched back to soda pop eight years later, ceasing its beer brewing.

Banner Brewing

Banner Brewing Company's beer label. *Courtesy of Stephen Johnson.*

The Banner Brewing Company existed from 1901 until Prohibition, but it did not have the usual humble origin story like many other breweries of this time. Banner was started when investors built a large, state-of-the-art brewery in Saginaw at Genesee and Pheolon Streets. It tried to stay afloat during Prohibition by making nonalcoholic drinks and renting out space to the Aero Cushion Tire and Rubber Company. The investors reopened after Prohibition's repeal, and they hired Fritz Goebel from the Detroit Goebel brewing family as head brewer. Hundreds of thousands of dollars were spent to update the brewing company, but pressure from the Detroit breweries, which were then shipping their products north, provided stiff competition. A delay in reopening (plus debt) put Banner behind other breweries. It just could not make and sell enough beer to be profitable and closed in 1938. Its assets were eventually sold to creditors.

Darmstatter

Louis Darmstatter started the Darmstatter Brewing Company in 1865, after his honorable discharge from the Union army. Louis brewed along with his son, changed the company's name to the Saginaw Brewing Company and grew his operation enough that he shipped his beer throughout the area. After Prohibition shuttered the brewery, locals bought the building, razed it and donated the land for use as Hoyt Park.

FLINT

The definitive history of Flint's brewing has yet to be written; however, its city directories tell some of the stories. In 1881, the directory listed several breweries that were up and running. The Central Brewery, with William Golden as proprietor, was located on Clifford Street between Kearsley and Union Streets. According to the 1894 directory, Golden was doing cooperage at this location—brewing is not mentioned.

The 1880s also saw William Lewis operating the Thread Brewery between Ninth and Tenth Streets. Edwin Green ran the Fenton City Brewery, with Christian Hux as his brewer (Hux was previously in business with William Wildanger, also spelled Willdanger, at their self-named brewery from 1874 to 1877). By 1894, Edwin was still living in the same location, but the nature of his business was unclear.

Flint Brewing Company

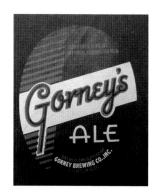

Gorney's Ale beer label.
Courtesy of Stephen Johnson.

By 1894, the Flint Brewing Company was the only brewery listed in the directory. Located at 2001 South Saginaw Street, the brewery was opened in the late 1890s (some sources say 1896, but the directory from 1894 lists it among the city's businesses) by William Wildanger, Robert Wisler and Adam Ketterman. It lasted until 1915, when Genesee County voted to go dry. After beer could no longer be brewed legally, the operation went bankrupt. The building was purchased by Methodists, who turned it into Lakeside Methodist Episcopal Church. At the time, this was seen as religious victory over alcohol. In later Prohibition years, it became a sign factory and then casket/ woodworks maker.

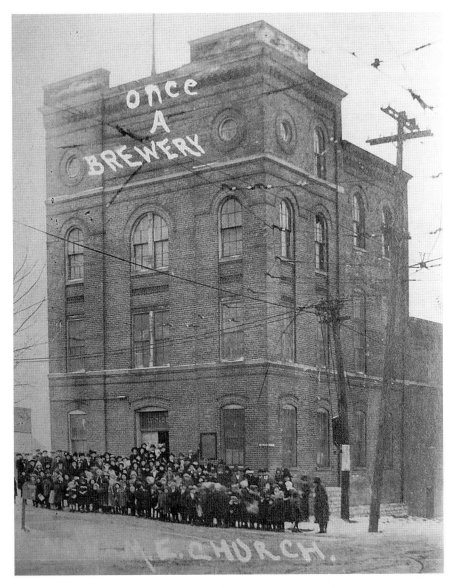

The former Flint Brewing Company building. *Sourced from Wikimedia Commons.*

After the repeal of Prohibition in 1933, Flint Hill Brewing Company bought the building, retooled it and began making beer again. It purchased the White Seal Brewing Company in 1939 and was absorbed by Valley Brewing in 1953, which later fell to the larger brands. The building housed a few other businesses before it was demolished in 1992.

The post-Prohibition years had more brewing activity, but these breweries had shorter lifespans: Gorney Brewing Company, listed at 920 Walnut Street, operated from 1935 to 1936; King's Tavern Brewing Company operated during 1938 and 1939; the aforementioned White Seal Brewing Company operated from 1939 to 1947 (when it was absorbed by Valley Brewing); and Frankenmuth Brewing Company had a facility from 1947 to 1948.

It is also mentioned in the archives that, in 1935, the sons of noted Detroit brewer Philip Kling bought the Dailey Brewing Company (reportedly only open in 1934) and operated it as Kling Brewery until 1947. Pfeiffer Brewing Company then bought it out and operated it until 1958.

CHEBOYGAN

Located at the top of Michigan's lower peninsula, the city now known as Cheboygan was originally settled by the Ojibwe. It got its current name in 1870 and was incorporated as a village a year later.

In 1872, the lumber business exploded in the area. That same year, the Hentschel brothers, emigrants from Prussia, bought land and began brewing on the western bank of the Cheboygan River. Within a year, their business expanded to brew five hundred barrels annually. They sold the brewery to German immigrants August Quast and Charles Schley in 1881, who continued to grow the operation.

A bit north on the river, James and Patrick Moloney built a brewery in 1882 and fittingly called it the Northern Brewing Company. Moloney arrived in the area from Detroit in 1876, working first in the grocery business. He was a village trustee who used his wealth to invest in his community, and he was especially committed to brewing only the best product (see sidebar for more).

The name was later changed to the Cheboygan Brewing and Malting Company when James bought out his brother's interests and production was increased to forty barrels a day. The company brewed brands like Silvo and Bohemian. In 1886, it began making drinks that were just becoming known as "soft," including ginger ale, cream soda, lemon beer and birch beer. It had locations in Sault Ste Marie and St. Ignace as well, and it always kept its line of soft and hard drinks fully stocked.

The brewery lasted until 1911, when it was possibly pushed out of business by the temperance movement and the growth of the lumber industry.

A closer look at the industry: the *Cheboygan Democrat* reported in 1888 an instance in which a reporter spent time with Mr. Moloney. The reporter learned his methods of brewing and malting. Moloney said, "The goods bearing [my] name should never be but the best that pure malt and hops could produce." Even during that time, "cheap beer" made by "unscrupulous manufacturers" could easily be made and sold. The paper gave some examples of the ingredients used to adulterate the beer: quassia, gentian, wormwood, alum and blue vitrol, nux vomica and even tobacco. These adjuncts offered bitter tastes, the presentation of a frothy head and more intoxicating properties. Moloney had a "standing offer of $5,000 to any person who can find any of the above adulterations in the beer they make…or anything else than the best of Canadian malt and pure hops."

ALPENA

In the 1850s, Alpena saw its first group of European settlers arrive. In the coming decades, their numbers grew, as the lumber mills opened and needed workers. Over nine thousand people called Alpena home in 1884, and they had two breweries to enjoy: Alpena Lion Brewery at Fourteenth Avenue and Chisholm Street and Alpena City Brewery at First Avenue and Chisholm Street, next to a vaudeville stage. There was also Lakeshore Brewing on State Street (which operated until it burned down in 1876), Union Brewing Company on West Chisholm Street and Pioneer Brewing Company.

John Beck opened Alpena Brewing Company in 1887, joining the other existing breweries, as well as over thirty saloons that served the city's ten thousand inhabitants. He added a three-story malting house in 1892 and changed the company's name to Beck Malting and Brewing Company two years later. The brewery produced silver foam lagers, export porter and bohemian export, as well as nonalcoholic beverages. The *City of Alpena, Brief Early History, the Present and Future* reported that the capacity of the brewery was twenty thousand barrels and that about two thousand barrels were always on hand, being kept cool in the cellar. The author

An advertisement in the city directory of Alpena. *From the city directory of Alpena.*

of the *City of Alpena* boasted of locals' preference for Beck's beer over any of the "famed beer" from Chicago or Milwaukee. The beer was met with the "appropriation of the best judges" and recommended by physicians as a "pure and health beverage, devoid of adulteration or any deleterious elements."

Beer fact: John Beck's home at First and River Streets was the only building to survive Alpena's great fire of 1872.

A true entrepreneur, Beck got involved with the thriving lumber industry and owned a saloon and hotel. He also didn't let two fires (one in 1901 and another in 1908) stop his beer from becoming local favorite. The thing that stopped him was Prohibition in 1918. The brewery did not reopen after Prohibition's repeal, and the building was a storage building until it was torn down in 1957.

Ionia

Grand Valley Brewing Company

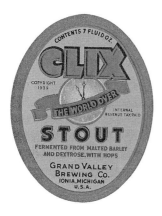

Grand Valley Brewing's Clix beer label. *Courtesy of Stephen Johnson.*

The city of Ionia can boast that its Grand Valley Brewing Company brewed the first malt liquor in the country. But did it? We do know that the brewery was owned by Clarence "Click" Koerber and that it produced several beers, including a malt liquor and a stout, using the "Clix" method.

While it is widely reported that malt liquor was first brewed around 1937 at Grand Valley Brewing Company, like with much local history, there are some questions about that claim. Some argue that Gluek in Minneapolis was the first, but just as many believe that it was Koerber. Gluek's grandson Alvin loved tinkering about in the laboratory and devised a way to make beer with less malt but with more of a kick. This was advertised as an upscale, more champagne-type of drink. Malt liquor then burst onto the scene, as Goetz Brewing, Gettleman Brewing and others began marketing it as a beer for refined, upscale postwar tastes.

Koerber began his operation prior to Prohibition and restarted it right after. The July 5, 1934 issue of the *Ionia Sentinel-Standard* heralded the reopening of the brewery after Prohibition. Koerber provided jobs in a community that desperately needed them, producing Friars Porter and a top fermented beer that was simply called Friars Beer. In 1937, the company introduced Clix Malt Liquor. In 1943, needing more space for production, Grand Valley purchased the Kern Brewery in Port Huron, renaming it Friars Ale Brewing Company. The brewery ceased operations in 1946, but the Port Huron facility kept on brewing until 1950.

Some Clix Malt Liquor labels were copyrighted as of 1939, but it is unclear whether this was meant to copyright just the name Clix or the entire name. (Gluek's malt liquor was trademarked in 1943.)

Part of the reason for these questions behind the origins of malt liquor is that the brewer Gluek called his Sparkling Stite "the original malt liquor." The brewery obtained a patent on the process of creating the malt liquor. Alvin went to the nation's capital and applied for a patent. According to

Friars Ale label. *Courtesy of Stephen Johnson.*

Gluek's records, the Stite beer received patent no. 2,442,806 on June 8, 1948. In the patent application, Gluek called his beer "the original malt liquor."

Was this done out of ignorance of Koerber's brew, or was it done in the hopes that the public simply would not know of Koerber's malt liquor? Was it done completely without malice?

Koerber made his malt liquor with the addition of sugar, and Gluek made his with a more complete fermentation process. So, perhaps it is six of one, half dozen of the other—Koerber used sugar, Gluek used a process that he eventually patented, and the world was left with an entirely new category of beer.

HURON COUNTY

The "Thumb" of Michigan boasts miles of beautiful lakeshores, charming small towns and water activities of all kinds.

Its original major beer supplier was what was sometimes informally called the Sebewaing Brewing Company, a local Michigan beer company that served the Michigan Thumb market. Officially known as the Huron County Brewing Company, it ran from about 1903 (when the *Sebewaing Blade* announced that it had built a sixty-barrel vat in their plant) until Prohibition in 1918. Six-packs of long necks cost a little less than one dollar, plus deposit. True to its German roots, the brewery offered an all-malt pilsner, lagers and bock-style beers.

On March 28, 1918, it advertised in the *Sebewaing Blade* its planned closure on May 1, indicating that supplies were running low and requesting that customers return bottles, cases and kegs. P. Pfaff was listed as the company's manager, and its phone number was simply listed as "21," asking for two rings to reach the company on its party line.

In 1924, local businessmen purchased the former brewing company and made malt extract with great success. After Prohibition's repeal, another group of businessmen stepped in and renamed the business Sebewaing Brewing Company. It made an old stock ale, Sport Beer and Gold Pheasant Beer. Local hunters seemed to appreciate the nod to their sport.

Top: The original wooden structure, circa 1893. *Courtesy of Scott Thede.*

Bottom: The Sebewaing Brewery, circa 1935. *Courtesy of Scott Thede.*

In the 1940s, the company purchased three young lion cubs from a circus and used this attraction to sell its beer. The lions traveled around that part of the state until 1948, when two were sold to a zoo and one was killed and mounted.

Michigan Brewery's beer label. *Courtesy of Stephen Johnson.*

The company continued brewing through the 1950s, remaining a relatively small operation, producing about thirty-eight thousand barrels per year. In 1960, its name was changed to Michigan Brewing Company in an attempt to appeal to areas outside of the immediate region. It model switched to producing "low-priced" beer, which also led to the use of low-price ingredients. The Buckeye Brewing Company moved to buy the brewery in 1965, but the attempt was stalled by a lawsuit from locals who objected to the "Sebewaing" brand being associated with Toledo. While the court proceeding did halt the sale, the brewery had already ceased its operations. It reopened but only lasted a few months before closing for good in 1966.

Archives list this brewery operating under a variety of names before Prohibition: Sophia Braendle Brewery in 1875, Veit & Graf, Henry Graf, Frederick Braendle, Braendle & Eberlein, Braendle & Kroll and Frederick Kroll Brewery.

MIDLAND

Midland Brewing Company was started in 1935 inside an old creamery located in downtown Midland. Its signature beer, known as Red Keg Ale, was named for the first lumber camp and saloon in the town. It did not survive the Great Depression, lasting less than a year.

Midland Brewing Company label. *Courtesy of Stephen Johnson.*

ADRIAN

Located in south-central Michigan, the city of Adrian is the county seat of Lenawee County. Its history includes prominent abolitionists, including the first congregation of Quakers in Michigan. They created a network of Underground Railroad stations in and around the local river valley. Village resident Elizabeth Margaret Chandler founded the Logan (then the village's name) Female Anti-Slavery Society in 1832.

The *Adrian Annual City Directory* listed several breweries in the late 1800s, many of which were started in 1874. The City Brewery at Railroad and Oak Streets made its way through the Fischer family, starting in 1874 as the Jacob Fischer Brewery, then changing hands to Joseph Fischer, E. Fischer and, finally, Catherine Fischer. It became Adrian City Brewery in 1898. It ceased operations in 1904.

Jacob Miller started his self-named brewery at Main and Broad Streets, eventually renaming it Eagle Brewery and continuing until 1877. The Star Brewery, with brewer Thomas Eason, started operating that same year at Main and Nelson Streets and lasted until 1879.

But preceding all of them by more than a decade was the brick building at North Main and Bristol Streets. Initially known as the Brick Brewery and likely built in or slightly before 1859, the brewery was started by a man named Joseph Pfeiffer. William Lehmann joined a few years later, and it became known as Union Brewery. When Pfeiffer left to take over another business, later running the successful Mineral Spring Hotel, Lehmann recruited Reinhold Kaiser as a brewer. Kaiser married William's daughter Anne and later took over the business for his father-in-law.

By 1882, the Adrian City Directory only listed the City Brewery (still in the Fischer family) and the Union Brewery.

Despite their reputation as rivals, Fischer and Kaiser built the Springbrook Brewery together on Maple Street in 1903. The workers in this four-story building made up to twenty-five thousand barrels of beer each year. Unfortunately, the temperance movement gained strength and put the brewery out of business in 1910.

CHARLOTTE

Charlotte Brewing Company had two runs—one from 1870 to 1884 and another from 1900 to 1909—with two different sets of owners, and it may have been used as a creamery when it was not a brewery. The brewery was located on Cochran Avenue, about a mile north of the courthouse. Stallnecker, Light and Bennett started the first iteration of the brewery, beginning with lagers but eventually focusing on ales and porters. Albert Henry Porter owned and operated Charlotte Brewing Company from 1900 to 1909. His death at the age of forty-two ended the operation.

HILLSDALE

In Hillsdale, John Haas (also spelled Hass) brewed from 1877 to 1893. While little is known about the brewery itself, there is a case from 1890 that shines little light on what happened to Haas. In the *People v. John Haas*, the brewer was charged with engaging in "the business of selling liquor without having complied with the provision of the law of 1887." Haas was tried in Hillsdale Circuit Court for "engaging in the business of selling and keeping for sale…malt, brewed and fermented liquors…without having paid his tax, posted his notice and filed his bond as required by statute." Haas's only defense was to allege defects in the prosecutor's case, and he was found guilty at trial and fined $200. But Haas appealed the conviction and ultimately prevailed when the Supreme Court of Michigan overturned and vacated the lower court's decision.

LAPEER

The Lapeer City Brewing Company was built in 1866 on Calhoun Street by John A. Buerger. The brewery was run by steam, brewing about two thousand barrels per year. The locals enjoyed the lager, which was also shipped out of state.

Buerger hailed from Bavaria, moving to the United States in 1850 when he was twenty-three years old. He landed in East Saginaw and later moved to Frankenmuth, where he involved himself in the business of brewing. He served in the Twenty-Ninth Regiment of the Michigan Infantry during the Civil War, earning the rank of first lieutenant. After the war ended, he moved to Lapeer to build the "city brewery" as well as the "Farmers' Home" hotel. His wife was Anna M. Szhelhms, and they had nine children:

Julianna, Christina, Barbara, Katherine, Theresa, Anna, John A., Oscar and Louisa. Buerger passed away in 1892.

Note: From 1891 to 1900, the brewery was operated under the name Anna M. Buerger Brewery before it became John A. Buerger again in 1901, probably operated by his son. Hollenbeck and Edmunds succeeded John A. Buerger in 1902 and carried on under the name Lapeer City Brewing Company until 1910.

Buerger's brewery's success was impressive, especially given that temperance movement started in Lapeer County as early as 1842. One of the first settlers in Almont attempted to start a temperance league shortly after he finished building his log cabin, but they moved on to nearby Romeo, which had whisky "as thick as mosquitoes."

By 1847, the county saw a "tidal wave of Sons of Temperance sweep over." Unfortunately, a man named Lyons started a brewery at the exact same time. A temperance lecturer, Moody, specifically railed against this enterprise. Despite this, local workers "drank the beer about as fast as they could make it." Nonetheless, when Lyons returned from a trip out of town and found the words "RAT SOUP FACTORY" painted on his building, he closed up shop immediately.

PETOSKEY

The "Old Brewery" was built in 1898, brewing Petoskey Sparkle Beer until 1915. The original owners were Frank and Garrett Fochtman, A. Bremmeyr and brewer John Zaiger.

The building stood four stories, or seventy feet, tall and twenty feet deep. It used gravity to move water and wort. Artesian wells on property provided the water and for cellaring and chilling; the company harvested ice from Mud Lake. In 1908, residents banned the sale of alcohol, only to reverse that decision in 1913, but in 1915, they voted to go dry again.

The building remained, but the brewery closed in 1915; at that point, it warehoused goods and later held retail shops. In 2012, Patrick Dowd and Lou Gostinger purchased the building and renovated it; it is now Petoskey Brewing Company.

Marine City

Taking up the entire block off Main Street, between Maria and Base Streets, was the Henry Heuser Brewery (also called the Joseph Heuser Brewery at some point). The business was owned and operated by Henry Heuser from the mid-1870s until his death either in 1897 or 1900. Some of the buildings were demolished in 1926 so that the new St. Mary's School could be built. During the school's construction, workers found a human skeleton in what had been the cellar of the brewery. Local doctors concluded that the remains belonged to Charles Wanke, a grocer and saloon owner who had disappeared in the early part of the century. Damage to the skull indicated that he had been struck with a blunt object.

An earlier report from the *Detroit Free Press* (August 5, 1879) indicated that before his disappearance Wanke and his brother had been in a saloon on Fort Street in the Springwells area. A man named August Mobias burst into the bar and engaged in "war-like conduct" with Charles, who, with his brother, gave a "shower of blows" to Mobias. The brothers were arrested but ultimately acquitted of the assault and battery charges.

Marshall

Marshall is the longtime home of Dark Horse Brewing Company, which was founded in 1997. Much earlier, in the spring of 1886, Joseph Gramer founded Marshall's first brewery. Assisted by his son Joseph Gramer Jr., Marshall made beer that was described as having "wholesome and health-giving quality, made of pure malt, as nearly like the home-brew as it is possible to make."

Rogers City

Paul Bittner came to Crawford's Quarry (now within the limits of Rogers City) in 1871, having worked with the Dueltgen family at their Flint brewery. An 1893 news article indicated that Bittner traveled to Chicago to attend the World's Fair. Bittner's brewery was known as the first brewery in Presque Isle County.

Bittner moved to Rogers City proper in the early 1900s, leaving his brewery in the hands of Henry Vietel, who later sold it to Fred Fisch. Fisch was a master brewer from Germany who worked in his native homeland and Detroit. The community of Crawford's Quarry disbanded in 1911, and Fisch was bought out by the Michigan Limestone & Chemical Company, which was expanding its calcite quarry. He received $1,300.

Paul Bittner was born in Germany in 1845 and died in 1932; he was buried in Rogers Township Cemetery in Rogers City.

WEST BRANCH

West Branch was incorporated as a village in 1885 and quickly established a bank, mill, creamery and brewery. The brewery, owned by Jacob Eck, existed under several names, including the aptly titled West Branch Brewery, during its years of existence (likely 1905 to 1910). It was advertised in the 1907 *Michigan State Gazetteer and Business Directory* as the brewer and bottler of pilsner, lager and export.

According to census records, Eck resided in Napoleon Township, Ohio, in 1900. Born in 1852 in Germany, he married a woman named Augusta and had two kids, Mary and Don; his stepchildren were Henry and Ida Schulty. Eck's occupation was listed as brewer. His 1907 advertisement lists his stepson, Henry W. Schulty, as his manager.

At some point, Eck switched from making beer to making soft drinks. (Eck possibly made this switch because, per the *Iron Mountain Press*, no saloons existed in West Branch as of at least 1915.) In 1915, the "pop works" owned by Eck was destroyed by fire; per the *Annual Report of State Fire Marshal to the Governor*, the cause of the fire was not known.

An earlier brewery was run in town by Anthony M. Schick from 1890 to about 1904. Schick passed away at the age of forty-six on September 22, 1904, and was buried in St. Joseph's Cemetery in West Branch.

WESTPHALIA

The first brewery in the town was opened in 1861 by Christopher Thiel, who emigrated from Lorraine, Germany; Thiel operated the brewery until 1866.

That same year, Peter Arens and Peter Thome began their own business north of town on Grange Road. This brewery was known at various times as the Clinton Brewery or Fritz-Cook Brewery. Given the state of the area's roads in those days, a board sidewalk was built between the town and the brewery. Local legend says that the boardwalk was "used quite a bit on most Sundays after church."

Later owners included Joseph Droste and then Fritz and Cook, who operated it until 1907, when Prohibition hit Clinton County.

OWOSSO

Gute

Brewing in Owosso began in 1855 with John Gute, who ran a brewery on Corunna Avenue. Originally from Wurttemberg, Gute settled in Owosso at the age of twenty-four and was up and brewing a year later. Within a decade, his place became known as the Owosso Brewery. By 1880, his son Albert had taken over the company's operations, producing two thousand barrels annually.

Gute Hill in Owosso featured caverns that were used to cool beer; later, Gute took advantage of the water on his property, opening a mineral bath company in 1871. With claims that the water was "health-giving," he saw people flock to his springs in the hopes of curing aches and pains, such as arthritis. Gute passed away in 1881, and the brewery closed a short time after that. By 1910, the spring was nearly dry.

Note: The Oak Hill Cemetery is across the street from the former location of the spring; some of that "health-giving" water possibly filtered through there.

Mueller

The Seiler Brothers/Roberts and Fletcher Grist and Flour Mill was transformed into the Owosso Brewing Company (Mueller Brothers Brewery) in the early 1890s. The Mueller brothers were natives of Germany, and their primary product was bottled export beer for local saloons, hotels and individuals. After the brewery burned down in 1898, the Mueller brothers rebuilt a one-story building and bottling house that they expanded in 1908. The brewery, located at 300 West Main Street, lasted until Shiawassee County went dry with a vote on April 4, 1910, which ordered saloons to be closed by May 1, 1910. Alcohol could still be found in the nearby village of Oakley to the north and Genesee County to the east.

COLDWATER

The brewery in Coldwater operated from 1867 to 1910 and changed owners and names several times. George Kappler operated it from its inception until he sold it in the 1890s. The last owner was named Benedict Doll; he was born in Bavaria, where he trained as a brewer. He came to the United States in 1883, brewing first in Ohio (where he married Emma Entenmann, with whom he had eleven children) and then coming to Coldwater, where he purchased Kappler's Brewery in 1894 (some sources say 1891 or 1899). Now called the Benedict Doll Brewery (and briefly the City Brewery), it brewed until Branch County voted to become "dry" in 1909.

Doll then sold ice and started a trash removal company. As more cars began traveling on the roads, Doll and his children ran a gas station, and his daughters Bertha and Marie later operated the Doll House Restaurant, near the former location of the brewery. Benedict passed away in 1941.

The Benedict Doll House Bed and Breakfast still stands at 665 West Chicago Street; it was occupied by Marie Doll until it was sold by the family in 1985. It is now a bed-and-breakfast. The brewery building still exists on West Chicago Street in Coldwater, although it has been used for many other things in the last one hundred-plus years.

MONROE

Jacob Roeder was born in Germany in 1835. When he was sixteen, he began apprenticing as a brewer and cooper. After immigrating to the United States at the age of eighteen, he landed in Monroe. In 1868, he built his hometown brewery and enjoyed quick success. Unfortunately, a fire destroyed the business in 1909 (although some reports say this occurred in 1907). The *Record-Commercial* reported that the "heavens were illuminated" when the brewery was believed to be struck by lightning. The main plant, a stone building, was deemed a total loss. The storage cellars were saved, as were some other buildings on the property. At the time of the article's publication, Roeder indicated that he intended to rebuild.

Rather than rebuild, Jacob became an agent for Stroh's Brewery. His son Herman did likewise, and the two built up the trade in the county. The *Jackson Citizen* made an observation at the time of the fire—that the county had voted to stay "wet," but its only brewery had been destroyed.

John Wahl also had a brewery in Monroe. Born in Bavaria, he originally trained as a mason. In 1861, when he was forty-one years old, Wahl left that line of work to open his lager brewery. He ran his eponymous brewery until 1882, when his nephew, also named John Wahl, assumed the company's operations. The brewery ran until 1905, when fire destroyed it. The elder John Wahl passed away in 1886.

PORT HURON

Brewing began in Port Huron in 1856, just a year before it became a city. A man known as J. Stein was the brewer. By 1863, the *Michigan State Gazetteer and Business Directory* listed two breweries in the area: one owned by Mrs. George Stein on River Street and another owned by Charles Sanberg (likely a misspelling of Samberg) on Michigan Street.

Later, John and John B. Billenstein produced lagers at the City Brewery and then the Union Brewery at Bard and Michigan Streets. This facility was purchased by Charles Samberg in 1874. Charles Samberg was known as the "dean of all brewers" at the time and brewed under his own name until about 1901, when the place became known as the Port Huron Brewing Company and carried on until Prohibition. Much later, the building was used for Port Huron's Lakeside Brewing Company, which was only around from 1936 to 1937.

Pine Grove Brewery existed around the time of Samberg's early days. It was owned by Albert Hendricks and John Russell and was located on River Street, opposite of Park and Bard Streets. The company made ale, porter and "Quinine Ale." The brewery was one of the largest industries in town in its heyday, but this distinction unfortunately did not protect it from tragedy.

Brewers were often leaders in their communities, and that was definitely true in Detroit:

» William Duncan served as an alderman, mayor and president of Detroit's City Council. Before coming to Detroit, he worked as a steward on steamers across the Great Lakes. A Democrat, Duncan began serving as alderman in 1852. After the city charter created the position of president, he served as the first president and then as the mayor in 1862 and 1863. Voters elected him to the Michigan State Senate in 1863. Detroit politicians asked him to run for mayor again in 1873, but poor health forced him to decline.

» Like Duncan, William Moloney was an alderman and city council president. Philip Kling was also an alderman and has the distinction of being the first president of Detroit's Brewers' Association.

» George C. Langdon was the mayor of Detroit. Born in New York, Langdon was sent to Flint by his father to be a farmer. He farmed for three years and then moved to Detroit to become a bookkeeper. After earning a master's degree in science for bookkeeping and accounts, he purchased his brewery in 1864; he later sold it to become a maltster. From these enterprises, Langdon amassed a personal fortune. A Democrat, he served as mayor from 1878 to 1879; however, his personal wealth was destroyed, and he had to take a job as a city hall clerk. It is not clear what caused his loss of money; the "Report on the Government of Detroit 1701 to 1907" simply says that he "experienced reverses, which stripped him of his wealth." At the time the report was written, in 1907, Langdon's eyesight was failing, but he was still on the job.

» August Goebel Sr. served in many capacities in his adopted hometown. He served as the superintendent of public parks, a representative in the Michigan State Legislature, a Detroit City Council member, the president of city council, the acting mayor and as the president of the waterworks' board.

A dock behind the building sat overlooking the Black River. Workers were coating beer casks for transport, using the standard, laborious practice of the day: putting some burning pitch into the casks and then corking them tightly. On this fateful day, Hendricks was present, overseeing his workers. He pulled an iron out of the fireplace and handed it to a worker, who put the iron on the cask without allowing enough time for the gas inside to escape. This caused a deafening explosion and sent workmen flying against the wall of the brewery. Hendricks was knocked off his feet after a piece of thick oak cover knocked him unconscious. Another piece of wood gashed an artery in his leg. Unfortunately, he passed away before help arrived.

Kern

Originally from Germany, Christian Kern arrived in the United States in 1870. In the 1870s (likely 1879, although some sources say 1875 or 1877), Kern took over a brewery on River Street that had been founded in 1856 and passed through several owners. In 1882, his buildings burned but were replaced within a year—only to burn again 1894. Nevertheless, Kern carried on, rebuilding over the remains. He employed over forty workers, brewing at a capacity of 200,000 barrels.

His successful brewery won the Paris Exposition's Grand Prize for its Cream of Michigan (also referred to as the "Michigan Cream Ale") Beer in 1911. (Many decades later, the Quay Street Brewery in Port Huron would base its signature ale on the Michigan Cream Ale from Kern.)

Kern's Cream of Michigan label. *Courtesy of Stephen Johnson.*

Kern Brewing Company advertisement. *Courtesy of the Library of Congress.*

The brewery soldiered on until 1919, when it was forced to make ginger ale and soft drinks instead of beer. It reopened after Prohibition, but like many others, it could not get find its earlier success. The brewery was sold in 1943 and renamed Friar's Ale Brewing Company. The buyer was none other than Clarence Koerber from Ionia. The Koerber family ran the business until 1950.

4

SOUTHEAST LOWER MICHIGAN

DETROIT

Alcohol has been part of Detroit since the beginning, and it was surely on the minds of the immigrants who arrived at the fort. Just a few years after the founding of Detroit, Antoine Laumet de La Mothe Cadillac imported a brewer by the name of Joseph Parent. Parent arrived in the new settlement in 1706 to make what was called a "small beer"—it had low alcohol content and was sourced from water of questionable quality, but it was still a fermented beverage.

In addition to being a brewer, Parent farmed and forged tools. In March 1706, he signed up to work for three years as a blacksmith for Cadillac and as a brewer for Detroit. Some historians believe that Joseph Parent had been living among Natives around what would become Detroit long before the arrival of Cadillac. According to a Detroit directory, Parent died in January 1710.

The new settlers created lives for themselves on ribbon farms, strips of land that extended from the Detroit River at a width of about two hundred feet, stretching up to two miles inland. These farms were free, in that no one had to "buy" the land, but they had rules to follow, including that they could not kill any rabbits, pheasants or partridges on their property, they had to pay a fee for the privilege of trading, they had to help assemble the maypole at Cadillac's home and that they could not assume a trade reserved for Cadillac's specially hired artisans, including brewing. In other words, Cadillac had the first monopoly on beer in the city.

It has been reported that Parent owned an enslaved person named Escabia. He was not the only early Detroit resident to own another human being. American history often omits the owning of human chattel in the North, so it needs to be noted that many of Detroit's settlers were owners of enslaved people. Cadillac himself owned one enslaved person, as did the city's first mayor, John R. Williams. William Macomb, for whom a county is named, owned twenty-six enslaved people who he ultimately willed to his widow when he passed away in 1796. That same year, a total of three hundred people in Detroit were enslaved. Joseph Campau and a commandant of the fort in Detroit, Jean-Francois Hamtramck, were also owners of enslaved persons, as were local priests. These priests encouraged newly arriving French immigrants to have their enslaved people baptized, lest they go to hell. Lewis Cass, the governor of Michigan Territory, and British naval commander Alexander Grant also owned human beings. The ownership of enslaved people in Michigan lasted until the 1830s.

If one was able to travel throughout time and take a trip around Detroit, they would see dozens of breweries. Most were not what we would consider a brewery today; rather, they were homes or buildings where people brewed. While space prohibits an exhaustive list of historical Detroit breweries, the following are some that one might see on his or her trip through time.

In the early 1800s, brewers had to malt their own barley if they did not want to pay to have bags of malted barley shipped to them. According to *Brewed in Detroit*, it is likely that local barley growers were early investors in breweries, such as Owens & Scott, believed to be the first brewery in Detroit. In 1831, these local growers advertised in the *Detroit Free Press and Advocate* that barley could be purchased for fifty cents a bushel and that customers could pick up said bushels at the "brewery opposite the Mansion-House, commonly called the Farmers Brewery of Detroit." Owens & Scott also advertised across the Detroit River in Canada, stating that porter beer and table ale were available for sale in both areas.

Thomas Owens was brewing at least a year prior. A fire in the *Detroit Gazette* offices on Griswold Street spread to nearby buildings, including the McDonnell

The "Old Mansion House," located on Bethel Street on the northwest corner of Atwater and Griswold Street, circa 1880. *Courtesy of the Detroit Public Library.*

house. In the cellar of the house, along with a hat store and auction house, were three hundred barrels of Owens's brew. The author of *Early Days in Detroit* stated that it was "a total loss" and that "beer ran down Griswold [and into the] street gutter nearly all the next day—a great chance for free lager."

Moving forward, one could find, circa 1836, Emerson Davis & Aaron Moore, located on what was then River Road (now Atwater or Fort Street). A year later, one would find it had moved to Woodbridge Street. Just a year after that, a second brewery, the City Brewery, could be found at Congress and First Streets. The fates of these early breweries are unknown; there is no mention of either brewery in the 1845 *Polk's Directory.* However, the 1850 *Polk's Directory* lists the Detroit Brewery at First Street, between Larned and Congress Streets, so it is possible that this was a continuation or reimagination of the City Brewery from years prior. Alexander King is listed as the brewery's engineer.

Today, concrete buildings and parking garages are located at Congress and First Streets, and the area around Woodbridge and Atwater Streets also contains many areas in which to park vehicles (that had not yet been invented when these early brewers set down roots).

Lager

In January 1848, a German brewer named Frederick Ams arrived in Detroit. He is credited with introducing lager to the city. (This calls into question the earlier quote from the author of *Early Days in Detroit* in reference to free lager; possibly, one could have enjoyed a free, albeit muddy, ale.) In later Detroit directories, Ams is listed as brewing at his home at 248 Maple Street.

There are no reports of Ams expanding beyond his home brewery into commercial buildings. Ams is listed in Jewish genealogical directories; it is therefore reasonable to assume he was a practicing Jew. There is no way to know whether his religion precluded him from expanding beyond his home operation; however, further mentions of Ams are scarce, which seems unfortunate, as it is believed he introduced lager to the new town on the river.

The Old Brewery

Hunt and June, the editors of *Early Days in Detroit*, described the "Old Brick Brewery" at the corner of Congress and First Streets as a "famous brewery in its day," when Thomas Owen, Curt Emerson, Josh Carew a man known only as "Carne," the aforementioned Davis and Moore, William Duncan and others operated it. Ale of the "finest quality" was produced at this location, which later became the site of the William Dwight Lumber Company. In their book, Hunt and June asserted that lager beer "came and knocked the heavy beers and ales out of the market," killing the old brewery. (From this description, it seems that Hunt and June are describing the City Brewery and the Detroit Brewery, both of which were identified as being situated at that location.)

Hunt and June also mentioned a Mr. McHoose, who had an "extensive brewery" on St. Aubin Avenue that was later operated by Carnes and Carew. Carnes was believed to be from London and was described as being "faultlessly dressed" around town—not so much while in his brewery. (Author's note: Nothing else about this mysterious Mr. McHoose was mentioned in the book, nor was he listed in the index.)

The editors of *Early Days* described Carew as a "bon vivant" who wouldn't dream of not being involved in promoting and organizing the social functions in the city. "A good fellow, ever ready to help the needy or assist in a charitable enterprise" with the wealth he amassed from his brewing. Curt

Emerson, a close friend of Carew, rounded out the group of partners. The three brewed for a time in the "old brewery" before being succeeded by William Duncan. At some point, Carew went to New York for a bit but later returned to Detroit.

The Detroit directories show no listing of anyone named Carew in 1856, so that could have been when he returned to New York; however, by 1860, Carew was brewing at the "Old Brewery," stating that he had "repurchased the institute for the dissemination of useful drinks and enlarged and rejuvenated it…making ale, porter and brown stout for draft and bottling, also selling to private families and consumers the Excelsior Cream Ale."

Early Days noted that Carew took hold of the brewery that "was where Dwight's Lumber Yard is now," making him the last to do business in the "Old Brewery."

Note: This is where the location comes into question. Dwight's Lumber Yard was next to Peninsular Dressed Lumber Company, which was at the southeast corner of Atwater and Riopelle Streets This differs from the earlier location of Congress and First Streets. It is possible that the lumber yard had multiple locations or that this was recorded in error.

The 1850s: Beyond the Old Brewery

Wherever its location, the Old Brewery was not alone in producing beer. In 1850, Henry Miller brewed at his self-named brewery, located at the southwest corner of St. Antoine, between Lafayette and Fort Streets. Like many of the early brewers, he worked close to home; the directory listed his "residence opposite" of the brewery.

The *Polk's Directory* listed both Thomas and Richard Hawley as brewers. Hawley's Beer Room was located under the corner of the Michigan Exchange on Shelby Street, selling "Cleveland Beer [and] a sandwich; nothing else." The editors of *Early Days in Detroit* opined that the "beer was fine…much better than Thomas Owen's brewery." Later, Hawley established his own brewery and malthouse on Bates Street, between Woodbridge and Atwater Streets.

Richard Hawley was born in 1815 in England and came to America at the age of three. By the age of seventeen, he was working with his father at the Cleveland Brewery, where he remained until the Panic of 1837, which caused his family to lose their livelihoods and personal fortunes. Richard left his adopted hometown in 1849, and within three years, he was brewing ale,

Duncan's Central Brewing delivery vehicle. *Courtesy of the Detroit Public Library.*

porter and strong beer on First Street in Detroit and then over on Bates and Jefferson Avenues.

Like so many others, Hawley began malting in 1855, likely because of competition from Duncan, who was the foremost ale brewer in those years. His sons Thomas, John and Richard Jr. joined the business, and Hawley retired in 1873. Two of his sons became lawyers after the Hawley Malt Company ceased its operations in 1884.

William Duncan opened his own brewery in 1850. Duncan's Central Brewery operated at 186–90 Woodbridge Street, west of Third Street. Duncan dedicated his trade to ale, advertising that the "medical faculty" recommended the brew to "invigorate the constitution." When ale sales started to decline, Duncan added malt making to his repertoire, operating under Duncan's Malthouse at 134–46 Beaubien Street, where he and his brother Ellison dealt in both malted barley and hops from about 1882 until 1895. Both Duncans made their home at 100 East Congress Street. As noted elsewhere, William Duncan involved himself in state and local politics.

Corktown

The Corktown neighborhood was home to brewer John Mason as of 1851. A small but mighty operation, topping out at six hundred barrels, Mason advertised that his beer was "always on hand" at his Michigan Avenue and Sixth Street operation and that he offered "superior amber and brown ales." Other Corktown brewers included Peter Bowker, John Blackmur and the Johnson family, who had emigrated from England in 1860. The last operator of the latter brewery was listed as Edward Johnson Jr., who listed the property for sale in 1888; by that time, the operation had fifty feet of frontage on Michigan Avenue.

Stroh

A brewery called Columbia was started by Michael Darmstaetter in 1852, located at 92 (later 227) Catherine Street. This brewery is notable for its location, which was just up the street from a man named Bernhard Stroh, whose place was located at 57 Catherine Street.

Many books have been written about this titan of beer; however, no Michigan beer history book would be complete without a least a look into the family and beer that were, for decades, synonymous with Detroit.

In the late 1840s, Germans, including Bernhard Stroh, arrived in town. The earliest Germans brewed lagers, coexisting with their English counterparts, who often made ale. Germans disdained the ales, because the lagers were more difficult to make, requiring more aging and precision. (Indeed, the word *lager* means "storage" or "aging" in German.) By 1860, about half of Detroit breweries were operated by Germans.

Bernhard Stroh was a third-generation brewer when he landed in Detroit in 1849. Just a year after arriving in a new country on a new continent, Stroh began producing Bohemian-style pilsners for his friends, neighbors and customers, brewing in copper kettles and peddling it door to door with a wheelbarrow. Initially, his operation brewed about ten barrels daily (about the capacity of microbreweries in the 1980s). He moved from his home operation to a new facility near Gratiot Avenue within the decade.

From 1875 to 1885, Stroh called his operation the Lion Brewing Company, using the heraldic lion emblem from the Kyrburg Castle in his native Germany. In 1875, he expanded his operation by constructing a campus for storing barley and hops, a facility for malting grain, a cooling house and a

Left: Stroh building. *Courtesy of the Detroit Public Library*.

Below: Unloading the Stroh beer! *Courtesy of the Detroit Public Library*.

The Stroh family, circa 1871. *Courtesy of the Detroit Public Library.*

family home. He changed its name to B. Stroh Brewing Company, operating under that name until his death in 1882 at the age of sixty.

Stroh's son Bernhard Jr. assumed control of the company at that time; in 1908, his brother Julius took over operations. By the time the new century rolled around, the Stroh Brewing Company was Detroit's largest beer producer at a rate of 300,000 barrels each year. Another rebuilding took place in the early 1910s, when the company added large, 250-barrel copper kettles to its production and began the fire brewing process that would become its hallmark. It was the last of the large breweries to use this traditional fire brewed technique.

The family-owned brewery changed its name to Stroh Products Company during Prohibition, making "near beer" (a nonalcoholic lager) as well as ice cream, soft drinks, "mixers" and malt syrups that were supposedly meant to be used by home bakers but were almost always used by home brewers. (Though the production of most of these items ceased when Prohibition ended in 1933, a special unit of the brewery continued to make Stroh's Ice Cream, which is still available today.)

Right after repeal of Prohibition, the brewery went on making beer as it had; its near beer was simply real beer that they put through a dealcoholizing process. Once it was legal again, it simply skipped the dealcoholizing and churned out its lager.

Stroh's operation, circa 1864. *Courtesy of the Detroit Public Library.*

Stroh's Lion Brewing Company, circa 1880. *Courtesy of the Detroit Public Library.*

Why did so many brewers also become maltsters? According to Brewed in Detroit, it is most likely because the ale market did not expand, and the little ale production that was happening was mostly being done—and done well—by Hawley and Duncan. Neither brewer switched to making lagers, because they knew how to make good ale, their customers enjoyed it and they simply may not have wanted to enter into competition with the Germans who were brewing lagers.

After Julius's death in 1939, his son Gari assumed the presidency. Gari's brother John succeeded him in 1950 and became Stroh's chairman in 1967. Gari's son Peter, who had joined the company after his graduation from Princeton in 1951, became president in 1968.

The company bought the Goebel Brewing Company in 1964, its first move toward expanding its operations. Stroh began targeting a national market, moving away from its reputation of being a local brewer. This move worked; by 1972, it was in the top ten of national brewers, and it moved into eighth place a year later. By 1978, Stroh's beer was available in seventeen states.

In 1979, the Stroh family bought the Parke-Davis Complex on the Detroit Riverfront, renaming it the Stroh River Place. In the meantime, the Stroh Brewing Company kept growing and buying other brands, including the F.&M. Schaefer Brewing Company and the Schlitz Brewing Company in 1982, becoming the third-largest brewery in the United States.

But the good times and good fortunes did not last long. Stroh's was Detroit's last operating brewery at the time it closed its doors. The tradition of brewing in Detroit temporarily ended on May 1, 1985, as the company closed its east side facility, saying it was the least efficient of its seven plants. The Cuyahoga Wrecking Co. imploded the historic Stroh's landmark on Gratiot Avenue a year later as thousands watched.

Competition and inefficient brewing processes at Stroh's other facilities caused the family to sell to Pabst Brewing Company and Miller Brewing Company in 1999. In 2016, Pabst Brewing Company partnered with Brew Detroit in Corktown to produce a Bohemian-style Pilsner. Stroh beer is currently available in cans and bottles.

1860s: Beyond Mr. Stroh

As Stroh's operation got underway, plenty of other brewers did the same. *Brewed in Detroit* quoted the *Detroit Advertiser*'s report that said there were more than forty breweries in the city in 1861; however, the Johnston City Directory only lists four "breweries": the aforementioned Carew and Duncan, as well as Minard's and Collins.

Minard's Brewery was located at the Thompson Farm on Michigan Avenue; in 1856, brewer/owner C.W. Minard was listed as a confectioner at 10 Montcalm Street.

The Collins' Brewery at Second and Abbot Streets advertised in local directories that the "taverns, hotels and private houses…highly [approved]" of its table beer, present-use ale and the "restorative stomachic tonic properties" of the Stock Ale. It boasted that all three were prepared from barley, malt and hops and referred potential customers to the "medical faculty" for analysis of its products.

By the 1860s, William Duncan was concentrating more on malting due to the lack of demand for ale. In 1864, George C. Langdon bought the Duncan plant, where he operated a brewery with Nathan Williams until 1872. Nathan Williams, one of the few to stick with ale, owned the Duncan plant next, and it lasted for another decade.

Other brewers included Charles Kunze, whose saloon and brewery were located at 48 Harriet Street; the Collins Brewery at Second and Abbott; the previously mentioned Frederick Ams, who was still brewing at 212 Russell Street; Eli Ruebelman, who brewed nearby at 262 Russell Street; John Dash, who brewed at 67 Adams Avenue; Ames and Schroeder, who brewed at corner of Clinton and St. Aubin Streets; William Darmstatter; Martin Vernor, who brewed in the Tenth Ward on Jefferson Avenue; Henry Seeley, who brewed at 358 East Lafayette Street; George Carne, who brewed at Atwater Street, near the waterworks; and F. Busch and Co., located at 59 Macomb Street.

Note: While only four official breweries were recognized in the official city directory, the names of individual brewers were listed, as noted previously. Likely, these were the people who were brewing out of their houses, and they may account for the remainder of the forty breweries indicated by the Advertiser. *The homebrewers in those days typically brewed for the blocks immediately surrounding their homes or some sort of saloon-brewery combination, where the saloonkeeper lived on the premises, brewing their beer in the back or in a shed.*

Late 1860s

Charles Endriss brewed at 350–52 Rivard Street beginning in 1867, just two years after arriving in the city. His daughter Elizabeth served as his bookkeeper. Other members of his family brewed as well, running their own operations.

Fred Grieser brewed at his home at Sherman and St. Aubin Streets beginning in 1871. He passed away just two years later, leaving behind his forty-one-year-old wife, Elizabeth "Eliza," and ten-year-old son, John. Eliza took control of the brewery, and within a year, she turned out over 1,200 barrels, increasing to almost 1,400 the year after. By 1876, Eliza was running a saloon out of the same establishment. Relatives (some reports say that they were sons of Fred) Louis and Nicholas lived in the house by that time, helping Eliza run the business; Nicholas worked with the Hawley Malting Company as well. In 1885, John Grieser was twenty-two years old and took control of the company, changing its name to Germania Brewing Company. John married a few years later, living at 193 Chestnut Street with his wife, Ellen. While it was small, the Germania Brewing Company delivered a decent living to the family, including Eliza, who passed away in 1895 at the age of sixty-four. Unfortunately, John died suddenly in March 1896; he was only thirty-three years old. Nicholas took over and brewed until the company closed in August 1898. A year later, Karl Zahringer and John Honer used the small plant to produce beer, but it only operated until 1900.

Working women were rare in the early days of professional brewing in Detroit. But in the case of the Endriss family, their daughter Elizabeth served as a bookkeeper. While not much else is known about her, census records indicate that she still resided in Detroit in 1940 at the age of seventy-one.

It was more common for the widows of brewers to become involved in the business, such was the case with Anna Kuhl and Eliza Grieser.

The Mann family had numerous relatives who brewed together and competitively. Jacob Mann opened a small brewery at 20 Maple Street with Gottlieb Endriss (the brother of Charles) in 1866, parting ways in about 1871. Jacob moved to the southwest corner of Rivard and Maple Streets to continue brewing under his own name. Gottlieb started his own business at 320 Rivard Street, brewing between 1874 and 1878. He brewed with his brother Julius for a time, later becoming a bottler who likely bottled his brother Charles's brews.

Christian Mann brewed out of his home at 278 Russell Street as of 1872, later moving to 2000 Gratiot Avenue and operating until about 1880. In the meantime, Lewis Mann brewed professionally starting in at least 1874 before opening a brewer's supply business in 1880.

Both Charles Endriss and Jacob Mann sold their interests to a British syndicate in 1889. August Goebel was placed in charge of these interests, and he was the one who closed both breweries a few years later.

1870s

By 1870s, the lager versus ale battles continued, as breweries classified themselves as either ale or lager brewers. There were many drinking choices at that time—dark Bavarian, pale Bohemian (lager), brown-black bock, brown stout and porters.

Anton Kuhl began brewing in the early 1870s, a small operation of maybe one thousand barrels, but it was enough to make a living. Anton died in 1874 by "reason of defective sidewalk" that was under repair by the city, according to the *Journal of the Common Council for the City of Detroit*. His widow, Anna Kuhl, carried on running the business, assisted by brewmaster Robert Kiessel. At some point during this time, the brewery was named City Brewing Company. In 1887, Anna sold it all to Joseph Nagel, who operated it under the name Westphalia Brewing Company at 425 Clinton Street.

Born in County Tipperary, Ireland, William E. Moloney arrived in the United States around 1855, coming to Detroit in 1862. He first operated a grocery store from his home at Twelfth and Howard Streets that he shared with his wife; by 1877, a brewery was also listed as part of the residence. His preferred styles of beer were English ale, porter and stout. By 1879, he had purchased a small brewery on Twelfth Street and added lagers to his repertoire, brewing golden Vienna lager and ultimately naming the plant

Westphalia workers. *Courtesy of the Detroit Public Library.*

Vienna Brewing Company. He still brewed ales and a porter under a label called Dublin Stout. His trademark was a hand holding up three fingers.

One brewery began in the 1870s at the corner of Abbott and Seventh Streets under the auspices of Rufus Brown, and it was called Western Brewing Company. It was listed by the *Advertiser* as one of the largest breweries in 1861; however, it was shut down in 1864, only to reopen a year later under new owners. When these owners moved east of Woodward Avenue to 630 Woodbridge Street in 1877, it became known as the East India Brewing Company. It advertised Farrell's Famous East India Pale Ale and Farrell's Old Country Porter, both of which were named for Brown's managing partner, Charles Farrell. Later, new owners moved the company again, this time to 621 West Fort Street; they dropped the east side/west side nomenclature and renamed the brewery Union Brewing Company.

August Ruoff became a "brewer by chance" after working as a silversmith. As a sideline business, he bought a saloon on Monroe Street, which led him to contacts with brewers. He began brewing four half barrels at home and prospered enough that he built a "proper" brewery at 335 Gratiot Avenue along with a saloon-residence, later adding both an icehouse and a malthouse. An advertisement in the 1875 city directory boasts of Ruoff's "celebrated lager beer" at 333 and 335 Gratiot Avenue, with free delivery to any part of the city.

Another brewery that was started in the 1870s was the Bavarian at 71 Sherman Street. It was started in 1874 by Anton Michenfelder; it was brewing up to five thousand barrels a year. Michenfelder advertised his beer as being made "exclusively from malt and hops…recommended by medical men, on account of its purity, as a wholesome tonic and strengthening beverage."

The 1875 city directory listed the Milwaukee Brewery, Julian Strelinger's Brewery and Saloon at 113 Bates Street (his residence) and 132 Griswold Street (saloon). The brewery of Ochsenhirt could be found at 148 Sherman Street around 1871; the operation changed its named to Home Brewing Company in 1890 before it closed in 1902. Additionally, Edward Johnson Jr. ran a brewery at the northwest corner of Sixth Street and Michigan Avenue and lived at 187 Sixth Street. John Scheu had his home, brewery and saloon at 351 Russell Street.

End of the Century

By 1880, ale brewers were in the minority. This switch was demonstrated by brewers like Thomas McGrath. Born in Dublin, Ireland, he came to United States in 1867, began work as farmer, moved into being a carpenter on a ship and ended up as a brewer. Like other Anglo-Saxon brewers, McGrath started brewing ale at his home at 98 Grand River Avenue but switched to lagers within two years. By 1891, he was producing ten thousand barrels a year, had a one-hundred-foot-long plant with refrigeration and its own steam power.

Of the twenty-eight brewers listed in the 1862 city directory, only a handful were still around in the 1880s. The largest was Duncan's Central Brewery on Woodbridge Street, which was still going strong under the auspices of Nathan Williams. Other prominent brewing families included the Klings, Martzes, Darmstaetters and Strohs.

This period is now looked back on as the Gilded Age in Detroit, as so many saloons and breweries existed for their thousands of customers. These brewers included W.E. Moloney, who carried on as the proprietor of the Vienna Brewery at corner of Twelfth and Howard Streets and then advertised himself as the "brewer of the celebrated Vienna Lager Beer"; the Martz Brothers Lager Beer Brewery and Bottling Works at corner of Orleans and Bronson Streets; the Mann family, who were still going strong;

Bavarian Lager Brewery advertisement. *Courtesy of the Detroit Public Library.*

and the Bavarian Lager Beer Brewery, operating at Rivard Street, not far from where I-75 is located today. And both Anna Kuhl and Elizabeth Grieser were still at it.

Other turn-of-the-century breweries listed the 1899 Detroit City Directory included some familiar names, like Bernhard Stroh, the Home Brewing Company at 142–48 Sherman Street, Kling Brewing Company at 1424 Jefferson Avenue, Columbia Brewing at 227 Catherine Street, Darmstaetter and Brother at 412 Howard Street, Greenway Brewing Company at 26 Cadillac Square, the East Side Brewery Co. at 34 Jay Street, Koch and Son at 129 Sherman Street, the Miller Brewing Company at 311 Woodward Avenue, Mutual Brewing Company at 617 Hastings Street, Nagle Brewing Company at 248 Mullett Street, National Brewery at 733 Hastings Street, West Side Brewery Co. at 412 Howard Street, St. Louis Brewing at 490 Grand River Avenue, the Voigt Brewing Company at 203 Grand River Avenue and Koppitz-Melcher's Brewing Company at 1115–125 Gratiot Avenue.

Koppitz-Melcher

Konrad Koppitz started his career strong as the brewmaster of Stroh Brewing Company. In 1890, he partnered with Arthur Melcher (who was related to the Stroh family by marriage) to begin a sixty-thousand-barrel operation on Gratiot Avenue. After Prohibition, it reopened with Ben Koppitz (Konrad's

Koppitz Victory Beer labels. *Courtesy of Stephen Johnson.*

son) at the helm. The brewery survived changes in ownership and a move to Dubois Street, near the Detroit River to produce Victory Beer and Black-Out Dark Beer during World War II. After the war, however, sales declined sharply, and it was sold to Goebel in 1947.

Voigt

Originally from Saxony, Germany, Carl William "C.W." Voigt came to Detroit via Wisconsin following the Civil War. While in Wisconsin, C.W. operated a small brewery in Madison. His only child, a son named Edward William "E.W.," worked and obtained knowledge of the industry at his father's Wisconsin breweries, where he worked in the winter, and in courses he took during the summer (as lager brewing was not possible then given the lack of refrigeration). E.W. attended public schools and later took business courses at the college level. The Voigt family moved to Detroit in 1864; there, Carl established another brewery in 1866. When he returned to his native Germany in 1871, C.W. leased the brewery to E.W.

E.W. opened the Milwaukee Brewery in 1872 at the age of twenty-eight. By 1877, the brewery was the second-largest producer in the city; in 1882, E.W. bought his father out completely and rebranded as the Voigt Brewing Company, winning four medals at the 1893 Chicago World's Fair for his Rheingold beer. Voigt's was among the breweries purchased by an

English syndicate in 1889; however, E.W. bought his business back in either 1895 or 1900 and brewed until Prohibition, when it became the Voigt Beverage Company.

E.W. became involved in Detroit and helped found the Detroit Art Museum, now the internationally known Detroit Institute of Arts. He also invested in the Edison Illuminating Company in 1866, employing a young chief engineer by the name of Henry Ford. Voigt turned his 150-acre farm off Woodward Avenue into the Voigt Park subdivision in the 1890s. At some point, Voigt also apprenticed as a sailor and captained his father's schooner. This well-lived brewer passed away in May 1920.

Kling

Peter Kling was born in 1818 in Kehl, Baden, Germany, and trained as a cooper. At the age of seventeen, he came to United States, landing in Detroit eight years later. Kling started a cooperage shop on East Woodbridge Street that did so well, he soon moved to a larger facility at Gratiot and Hastings Streets. (It is possible that a young brewer named Stroh bought his barrels there, but this has not been confirmed. What is confirmed is that Kling did a lot of business with a man named Hiram Walker.)

In 1856, along with shoemaker Michael Martz and store owner Henry Weber, Kling bought property near the future location of the Belle Isle Bridge (between East Jefferson Avenue and the Detroit River). The Peninsular Brewery was born, with Gottlieb Frankenstein as its head brewer. The barrels were made by Kling himself for the first ten years of operations. Kling began assuming more control over the facility, and after Henry died, his widow, Caroline Weber, took his place as a proprietor until Kling bought out her interest and incorporated the business into Peninsular Brewing Company; eventually, the operation became known as the Philip Kling Brewing Company.

During this time, Detroiters could enjoy brands such as the Pilsener, Porter, Extra Pale Ale and Gold Seal Export. After a fire in 1893 devastated the facility, the company constructed a six-story brewhouse that continued satisfying patrons around the city.

While engaging in the business of beer, Kling served as an alderman in Detroit and as the inaugural president of the Detroit Brewers' Association. With his first wife, Margaret, Kling had daughters who were not considered as viable brewery workers because of their sex; however, he did hire his

Kling Brewing Company. *Courtesy of the Detroit Public Library.*

oldest daughter, Julia, as a bookkeeper and listed her as the secretary-treasurer of the company. Kling and his second wife, Josephine, had more children, including a son named August, who ran the brewery with his father. The Klings' younger son Kurt studied business at the University of Michigan and took a brewmaster's course in brewing science in New York, ultimately becoming a brewmaster and superintendent at his dad's business. Philip Kling retired at the age of eighty-two in 1900. It was reported that Kling was often shy about being known as a brewer, preferring instead to be thought of as a cooper.

In 1906, the *Western Brewer* reported that at the age of eighty-seven, Kling was thought to be the oldest surviving brewer in the country who was still able-bodied and of sound mind. Philip passed away in 1910 at the age of ninety-two. His widow, Josephine, became the president of the company, and his son Kurt served as the general manager.

Kurt Kling carried on until Prohibition, when the company became known as Kling Products Company. It operated until 1921, and the building was torn down in 1923.

But that is not all Kurt did—he also ran an amusement park. First known as Electric Park and located next to Kling Brewing, the park opened on May

Kling Brewing Company. *Courtesy of the Detroit Public Library.*

26, 1906. While some sources indicate that Kurt built the park, most report that Arthur Gaukler, a prominent insurance salesperson in the city, built the park after visiting similar ones around the United States and Europe. The *Detroit News* raved about the grand opening performances of Great Chick, a "tramp cyclist and comedian" and the "funniest man on wheels." Later, the park featured aerialist Mademoiselle Patrice, who performed a "thriller," descending from a platform using the "Spanish web." Also featured were rides powered by electricity; an interactive model of the 1889 Johnstown Flood; pavilions for dancing, bands and concessions; and the "Inferno," which promised a trip through Dante's underworld. The park ran for twenty-one years and became known as Luna Park. Late in its existence, it was operated by Kurt Kling. Sadly, the city condemned many of the park's rides and buildings in 1927, and it was all torn down the following year. A public park named for Father Gabriel Richard took its place.

But things were not over for the Kling family. After the repeal of Prohibition, Kurt Kling bought the Daily Brewery in Flint and began brewing again in 1936, lasting until 1942. Pfeiffer Brewing Company (started by a former engineer at Peninsular, Conrad Pfeiffer) bought the vacant building in 1947 to manufacture draft beer. It operated at this location before closing for good in 1958.

Note: And still, the brewing tradition continues, albeit in Florida. The great-great-great-grandson of Philip Kling owns a brewery in Tampa's Ybor City known as BarrieHaus Beer Company.

Cooperative Brewing

These aforementioned larger brewers posed a threat to the smaller, home-based ones. For instance, cases could be delivered directly to people's homes by the larger breweries, whereas the smaller ones, unable to afford the cost of bottling, could only offer kegs to local saloons. Additionally, before Prohibition, it was not uncommon for American breweries to own saloons where they sold their beer to a steady stream of customers. Often, this did not please saloon owners, who were using a variety of beers on their taps and therefore paying a variety of prices that were set by the brewers. Likewise, this caused financial problems for smaller breweries that did not have the capital to buy their own private taverns. All around the country, these entrepreneurs solved this problem by putting their money together, buying small breweries and then hiring brewmasters to make beer for them. Now that they were part-owners in breweries, they could control the prices.

In Detroit, four breweries tried this cooperative experiment: Union Brewing Company, the East Side Brewing Company, Independent Brewing Company and the Mutual Brewing Company.

The Union Brewing Company name was revived in 1888 for a new venture located at 24 Mitchell Street and headed by Joseph Aiple, the former brewmaster with Goebel. (This does not appear to be related in any way to the previously mentioned Union Brewing Company that succeeded the East India Brewing Company.) Independent Brewing Company was located on Central Street, near West Warren Avenue. It was formed by thirty saloonkeepers in southwest Detroit, who collectively got fed up with the position held by breweries. They served the Springwells District, offering choices and choice prices to the member saloons. Serving the east side was the aptly named East Side Brewing Company, located at 468 Gratiot Avenue; it brewed until about 1904. The Mutual Brewing Company was organized in 1894 by mostly saloon owners, and while it featured no mechanical cooling operation, it managed to provide beer for its members until 1915.

Later, the Union Brewing Company did reopen with different owners and a different name (Cadillac Brewing Company), but at that time, it found itself as one of many small breweries trying to compete with larger companies.

The interior of Independent Brewing Company, circa 1911. *Courtesy of the Detroit Public Library*.

During this golden age, many brewers were of German and English descent; however, several brewers of other nationalities came onto the scene in the late 1800s and early 1900s. Names like Goebel, Chronowski and Zynda—a major Polish brewer—pushed onto the market. This corresponded with the beginning of consolidation and pasteurization, as big brewery owners realized the only way to compete was to produce large volumes.

The Chronowski brothers brewed at their Auto City Brewing at 8214 McDougall Street from 1910 to 1941. Popular with Slavic employees around the Dodge Main Plant, the company brewed up to forty thousand barrels a year by 1914. The brothers sold home brewing supplies and liquid malt during Prohibition. Some of their other relatives were busy as well. Their brother Joseph, who had learned a lot about financial systems while running a brewery, organized the Liberty State Bank during Prohibition. Another relative continued brewing on the sly—and served time in prison because of it. *Brewed in Detroit* says that the Chronowski family owned a building that they leased to this unnamed relative; after a raid, the family was in the clear, but the "front man" had to spend some time behind a different kind of bars—those of Leavenworth Prison. The family legally brewed again after Prohibition's repeal, making seventy-five thousand barrels a year until 1937. But the local economy took a nosedive, and the family did not escape unscathed. Their brewery closed for good in 1941.

Other Polish-owned breweries included Wayne Brewing Company at 3603 Hancock Street in Detroit, which opened after Prohibition's repeal but only lasted for four years, and Thomas Zoltowski's brewery at 733 Hastings Street (Zoltowski originally operated a drover store from his home at 743 Hastings Street but turned it into a saloon and then brewed nearby from 1891 to 1919).

John Zynda opened White Eagle Brewery in 1886. Zynda learned how to brew in East Prussia and later in Detroit as a foreman at Michenfelder Brewery. His beer was extremely popular in his hometown of Hamtramck—and this proved the old axiom that it's good to have friends in high places, as his political connections allowed him to thwart Prohibition raids at his Macomb Street plant. His brewery lasted until 1948.

In the 1890s, emigrants from Belgian began arriving in Detroit, brewing their own creations. Frantz Brogniez opened the Tivoli Brewing Company on the east side of Detroit on Mack Avenue in 1898 with financial help from local Belgian leaders. Around 1910, the company began brewing Altes (meaning "old" in German), which was a beer "specifically crafted for the

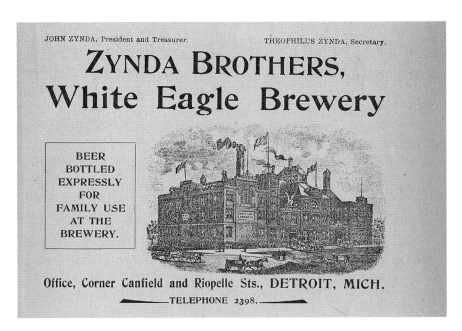

Zynda advertisement. *Courtesy of Stephen Johnson.*

Tivoli Brewing Company label. (What's the answer to the riddle?) *Courtesy of Stephen Johnson.*

automotive industry" and later advertised as a beer for the working class. The traditional Bavarian-style lager joined the wave of lagers that continued to grow in recognition. While beer production was shut down during Prohibition, the brewery survived by selling malt syrup and carbonated beverages. Tivoli Brewing Company reopened in 1933, quickly growing to produce 400,000 barrels a year in 1936. By 1948, the Altes brand was so popular that the brewery changed its name to Altes Brewing Company.

Over the course of the next decades, the company was acquired by the National Brewing Company, the Carling National Brewing Company and finally the G. Heileman Brewing Company, which continued to brew Altes in the city until 1971, when it closed the Detroit facility and moved its production to its brewery in Frankenmuth.

Heileman was then acquired by the Stroh company in 1996; in 1999, when the Stroh Brewing Company was sold to Pabst, it still owned the Altes brand. The brand disappeared but made a reappearance in 2019. Once the official sponsor of the Detroit Lions and Detroit Tigers, the beer reemerged on the Tigers' opening day at Nemo's Bar and Grill in Corktown. Altes Original Detroit Lager also hit the shelves of stores and the mugs of restaurants that year. A local restaurant called Traffic Jam and Snug also introduced the Altes Sportsman, a Vienna-style lager brewed by Brew Detroit.

Prohibition and Everything After

From the time Michigan became a state in 1837, people wanted to make it a dry state. Groups that pushed for statewide alcohol prohibition decried this "home rule" law, and groups like the Women's Christian Temperance Union, Washingtonian Society and the Anti-Saloon League rallied and lobbied for temperance at both the state and local level. In 1845, Michigan became the first state to allow individual municipalities to decide for themselves whether to prohibit alcohol. Michigan had its first era of prohibition from 1855 to 1875. Some areas took it seriously, but others simply did not enforce the law. By 1875, so many cities were openly defying the law that it was dissolved. Attempts to reenact prohibition took place in 1877 and 1879, but they were not successful.

The temperance and prohibition advocates soldiered on. Carrie Nation paid a visit to the state in 1908, haranguing the governor and smashing up the bar in the Holly Hotel. By 1911, about half of the mostly rural state was dry, but Detroit remained a hard-drinking town. While the *Michigan Catholic Magazine* urged voters to vote "against the saloon," most of the temperance movement was led by Protestant evangelicals. Evangelistic preacher Billy Sunday spent much of the 1916 election season in Detroit, rallying, preaching and passing his collection plate. The nation's entrance into World War I stoked a wave of anti-German sentiment, allowing xenophobes to campaign against the city's German American brewers. On November 7, 1916, voters approved the "home rule" or "local option," which allowed each municipality to decide for itself whether wanted to prohibit alcohol.

Michigan voted to go "dry" about two years before national prohibition took effect, on May 1, 1918. This meant that the manufacture, sale and transportation of alcohol was prohibited in Michigan, but the private, in-home drinking of beer and other alcoholic beverages that had been purchased before May 1 was legal.

Thankfully, that "noble experiment" ended in 1933 with the passage of the Twenty-First Amendment. Within a year of Prohibition's end, a dozen breweries were on the scene in Detroit. Some were new upstarts, others were upgrading their old plants and still others were just in their initial planning stages. These new breweries included the Von/Kraft/Kraftig Brewing Company at 1800 East Forest Avenue, which was started from scratch and staffed by a brewer with over forty years' experience, Matthew Stegmeyer. There was also the Michigan Brewing Company at 1262 Military Avenue, Old Holland at 563 East Larned Street and Regal Brewing Company at

Exposition Brewing Company in Del Ray. *Courtesy of the Detroit Public Library.*

Walker Brewing Company in Center Line. *Courtesy of the Detroit Public Library.*

3220 Bellevue Avenue (designed by Harley-Ellington, who constructed much of Stroh's post-Prohibition designs).

The brewery at 1000 Cary Street, near the Delray community, had several names, including Exposition/American/Chase and Mechanic/American Brewing Company of Michigan. The company was known for its Cream Top Old Style Lager until Prohibition, which it rode out under the name American Products Company. It sold birch beer and ginger ale but closed in late 1938 due to declining sales.

Wayne Products and Brewing Co. got its start during Prohibition by making and selling liquid malt, a still-legal necessity for thirsty home brewers at the time. Once Prohibition was repealed, the folks behind Wayne got their own brewing business up and running, but it didn't last long. The company was shuttered for good in 1937.

Outside of Detroit proper were C.&K./Wagner Brewing in Hamtramck; Imperial Brewing Company, which was opened in Ecorse (about twelve miles south of Detroit proper) by William Bache; and Walker Brewing Company at 8561 Center Line Street. For the latter, lower land values in this separate community may have been the attraction for brewer John George Walker.

Note: The recession in 1937 curbed individuals' incomes and their purchase of beer. Of the twenty breweries that were in business in 1934, only twelve remained in business a year after the recession. Dominating the local market were Stroh, Pfeiffer, Goebel and Tivoli, Schmidt, E.&B. and Detroit Brewing Company (Martz). In the decades after World War II, Detroit breweries boiled down to the other "big three"—Stroh, Goebel and Pfeiffer.

Martz

Three brothers came to Detroit from Germany in 1839 and opened a brewery. Michael Martz and his brothers Frank and John called their business Continental Brewery and built it up at Orleans and Bronson Streets (now Adelaide Street). When they relaunched as the Detroit Brewing Company in the late 1870s, the brothers saw the sales of their ales soar. It was their lager, Oldbru, that became the best seller, and the brand that was revived after Prohibition's repeal. The second generation of Martzs grew the company's production to 200,000 barrels during World War II, but sales fell significantly after the war's end, and the brewery closed in 1948.

Detroit Brewing Company delivery vehicle. *Courtesy of the Detroit Public Library.*

Detroit Brewing Company beer label. *Courtesy of Stephen Johnson.*

Ekhardt & Becker (E.&B.)

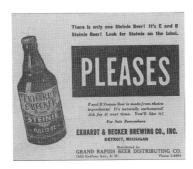

E&B advertisement. *Courtesy of Stephen Johnson.*

As noted elsewhere, John Koch started the Ulmer Brewery in 1872, selling to August Ekhardt and Herman Becker in 1883. With experience brewing for both Stroh and Kling, Ekhardt moved in quickly, renaming the company Michigan Brewery and purchasing competitors as it gained a growing share of the market. Just prior to Prohibition, the brewery, then known as E.&B., had a production capacity of sixty thousand barrels.

After Prohibition's repeal, the families retained the company but left the actual managing to professionals, who ultimately grew the company to a production capacity of 244,000 barrels. In 1952, it acquired the Schmidt Brewery, selling E.&B. Beer and E.&B. Golden Ale, in addition to Schmidt recipes. In 1962, Pfeiffer bought E.&B. and the brand ended there.

Schmidt

The brewery on Wilkins Street began in 1872 as the George Hauck Brewing Company. The name changed a few times (Hauck & Bauer, Hauck & Kaiser, Champion) before Joseph Kaiser and Frank Schmidt took over in 1895. They saw success, brewing thousands of gallons a year. By becoming the Schmidt Products Company in 1919, the brewery made it through Prohibition as a company. It began brewing again after Prohibition's repeal, canning its beer in cone-topped cans that boasted "no sugar" and "no glucose" in the "natural beer." The company enjoyed strong sales at first, but postwar competition proved to be too much, and it ceased operations in 1951. The brand was acquired by E.&B. a year later.

Pfeiffer

Conrad Pfeiffer was born in Calderon Kreiss, Marburg, a province of Hesse-Cassel, Germany, in 1854. The *History and Biography of the City of Detroit and*

Pfeiffer's Famous sign. *Courtesy of the Detroit Public Library.*

Wayne County, Michigan described him as a "scion of families long established in that favored section of the empire." At the age of seventeen, Pfeiffer came to America, landing in Detroit soon after his arrival; there, he became an apprentice as a locksmith and machinist, working for a time at Riverside Iron Works. He began working as an engineer at the Peninsular Brewery for Philip Kling in 1881, staying on for three years, and after this, he became the engineer of the Charles Endriss brewery.

In 1902, Pfeiffer began organizing his own venture, incorporating the C. Pfeiffer Brewing Company. Pfeiffer's brewhouse was located on the east

Pfeiffer Lunch Recipes booklet. *Courtesy of the Detroit Public Library.*

side, between Beaufait and Bellevue Streets along Mack Avenue. He brewed Wurzburger, export and a lager called Pfeiffer's Famous Beer. The company was strong enough that Conrad purchased a city block with a rail line so that his beer could be shipped outside of the city.

Pfeiffer was a member of the National, Michigan and Detroit Brewers' Associations and the Detroit Board of Commerce, and he owned real estate throughout the city. He was described as "genial and courteous," with a "wide circle of friends in both business and social lines." He married Louisa Cramer and had three sons (all of whom died as children) and two daughters.

Pfeiffer died in 1911 at the age of fifty-seven, so his wife, Luisa, and daughter Lillian assumed control of the company's operation as president and vice-president, respectively. The company brewed beer until Prohibition.

A new firm that used the same name but involved no members of the Pfeiffer family began brewing again in 1934. Alfred Epstein, a brewer from Austria, ran the company, expanding it to encompass most of the block and adding a bottling facility and office building, ultimately brewing 400,000 barrels in the 1940s.

The firm did well with the regulations put in place by the government during World War II. The brewery flourished, sending olive-colored cans to troops overseas. The cans featured the Johnny Fifer mascot, designed by the Walt Disney Studios. The jaunty fellow proclaimed that the famous beer "follows you around the world in this special overseas can." The taste for this beer followed the servicemen when they returned home (see sidebar).

Unlike many other breweries, which saw sales decline after the end of World War II, Pfeiffer's annual production grew to over 500,000 barrels; at one time, it surpassed even Stroh and purchased Kling Brewery of Flint and Jacob Schmidt Brewing Company. The brand, the best seller of Michigan during the 1950s, held strong until the end of that decade.

Johnny Pfeiffer! *Courtesy of Stephen Johnson.*

The Detroit brewery worker's strike of 1958 began Pfeiffer's decline and led to its decision to become a regional brewery. In an attempt to compete against the giant national brands, the company renamed itself Associated Brewing Company with the goal of acquiring multiple local brands with proven strong sales. After buying breweries from Illinois, Indiana, New York and Massachusetts, Pfeiffer became the tenth-largest brewery in the country. Its headquarters remained in Detroit, and it remained profitable, but competition with national brands damaged the company. The plant on Beaufait Street closed in 1966, when the owners moved to Indiana as a cost-cutting measure. Heilman Brewing Company purchased the Pfeiffer name in 1972 and was itself bought by Stroh in 1996.

Goebel

August Goebel, an emigrant from Prussia, set out for Chicago but ran out of money before he got there. He settled into working at a bookbindery in Detroit and served in the American Civil War, rising through the ranks to become a captain.

After completing his service, he partnered with Theodore Gorenflo in the A. Goebel & Company Brewery in 1873. It started strong with its extremely

The United States government directed all breweries to allocate 15 percent of their products to members of the military—basically guaranteeing that servicemen would receive beer. The government also compelled breweries to stop canning, except for shipment to the troops who were serving overseas; all other products had to be bottled or kegged.

This requirement had an unintended side effect for breweries, as they could then promote themselves as patriotic, making nutritional beer, chock-full of that vitamin B–rich yeast. This led to a rebranding public relations campaign to undo the damage done by decades of temperance and the years of nationwide Prohibition. Breweries were able to demonstrate that they were essential businesses that paid taxes, donated products and were necessary for the war effort. The government agreed, proclaiming brewing an essential wartime business.

Servicemen were allotted rations of beer brewed to 3.2 percent ABV (a nod toward the politicians who still represented "dry" areas of the country), and this beer was issued on ships or sold at the post. The servicemen developed a taste for the German-style lager that they drank during the war, and after returning home, they sought out similar beers, helping pave the way for the dominance of the Pabst, Coors, Anheuser-Busch and Miller brands.

World War II affected much of the beer industry in Detroit, with manpower and raw materials shortages. However, the desire for the product did not diminish, leading to some shortcuts in the process, the easiest being brewing thinner beer. Arguably, customers did not mind, as many lined up at stores with their empties, grateful for whatever brand was available.

popular German-style dry lager, and by the 1880s, it was the third-largest brewery in Detroit, only behind Voigt and Kling. Part of the reason for their size was that Goebel consolidated the Michenfelder, Mann and Bavarian Breweries into one company.

The brewery moved to a new facility at Rivard and Maple Streets in 1879 and expanded several times in the 1890s, producing beers like a dark Wurzburger, Pilsners and a low-alcohol malt tonic.

Above: An early 1900s Packard serving as a Goebel delivery vehicle. *Courtesy of the Detroit Public Library.*

Opposite: Goebel's building. *Courtesy of the Detroit Public Library.*

Goebel passed away in November 1905, at which time, his son August Jr. took over the business. He continued to grow the brewery and began distributing the beer. By 1909, it was brewing sixty thousand barrels a year. More expansion was planned, but Prohibition halted these plans, leading to the dissolution of the company.

Goebel began production again in 1934. Because of the original logo's similarities to a symbol appropriated by the Nazis, Goebel changed its "thunder eagle" to a bantam and then changed its name to Brewster the Rooster in the 1950s. This mascot grew in popularly—as did Goebel beer. At its peak, it produced 1.3 million barrels a year. Along the way, it purchased the Grand Rapids Brewing Company in 1946, Koppitz-Melchers in 1947 and a California brewery in 1950.

Just as the company was planning more expansion, its workers went on strike for almost two months in 1958. At the same time, out-of-state beer sales rose to take up 42 percent of the market. These events combined to

flatten the sales, such that by 1964, the company was sold to Stroh, which continued to market the brand. After Pabst acquired Stroh, it likewise continued to use the Goebel name until 2005.

BLACK BOTTOM

On the east side of Detroit was a residential area known as Black Bottom (so called because of its rich soils; historically, the area was part of a riverbed that was buried to be used as a sewer in 1827). Bordered by Gratiot, Brush, the Detroit River and the Grand Truck railroad tracks, it was one of the few parts of Detroit where Black residents were allowed to live. Racist policies— including a literal wall on the northwest side of the city, near Eight Mile Road—prevented integration among the races. Paradise Valley was located north of Gratiot, an overlapping neighborhood that was the business district and entertainment center of these communities. Over three hundred Black-owned businesses cared for the residents—from restaurants to golf courses and drugstores. Entertainment came in the form of bowling alleys, theaters and nightclubs, the latter of which featured the greats of the day, such as Billie Holiday, Duke Ellington, Dizzy Gillespie, Ethel Waters, Pearl Bailey and Ella Fitzgerald.

It was here that Reuben Ray began a beer distribution company after Prohibition's repeal, with a focus on distributing to the city's Black population. In 1938, Paradise Valley Distributing Company was in operation, and it is reported to be the first Black business of its kind in the country.

The *Detroit Tribune* proudly announced the opening of the "real, honest-to-goodness beer distributing agency with [Black employees] from the front office to the mop man…owned and operated by [Paradise Valley] people." At the time, Ray was already known as the only distributor of coin

The 1958 brewery workers' strike involved five breweries (Stroh, E.&B., National, Pfeiffer and Goebel) and locals 3 and 38 of the Brewing Workers Union and local 181 of the Bottlers Workers Union.

The strike lasted about two months and is often accused of nearly putting the Detroit breweries out of business. Some reports blame the strike for allowing national brands, such as Budweiser, to get a foothold in the city.

The brewery workers' contract expired on April 1, and the issue boiled down to what the retroactive pay date would be. This was a relatively minor issue in the grand scheme of things, but it became a sticking point.

The union brought its list of proposed contract changes to the brewers on April 12, with the request that the agreements in the contract (including pay) become retroactive to April 1. The brewery owners insisted on retroactivity to April 15 instead of the date the contract actually ended on. Since the contract had then expired, the 4,500 workers walked out.

The strike lasted until May 20. Ultimately, state and federal mediators were brought in, and they entered a fourteen-hour-long bargaining session that led to a three-year contract—that didn't even mention the retroactivity.

phonograph machines, or jukeboxes; a promoter of prize fights; and an early supporter of Joe Louis.

His entrepreneurial spirit gave him great success by the time he opened the distributing company. Starting with one truck and one small shop on Beacon Street, he soon acquired larger quarters and more trucks. By 1941, the *Detroit Tribune* reported that twenty-two Black employees were on his payroll.

A pamphlet from 1940 shows that the company was distributing Friars Old Stock Ale, Risdon's Wines, Koppitz Silver Star Beer and Clix Malt Liquors. The company's local focus was evident in its slogans, which included "Help make jobs for colored men and get more for your money" and "Building employment for negro youth."

So called "urban renewal" programs in the 1960s ended life in the Black Bottom. Paradise Valley was destroyed in 1959 as the I-375 portion of the Chrysler Freeway went up. Local Black people were forced to scramble to find places that would allow them to live their lives. Some found property in a formerly Jewish neighborhood on Twelfth Street; others were not as lucky. What was once a thriving area for Black people is now partially occupied by Ford Field and Lafayette Park.

Outside of Detroit

Fort Dearborn

Edwin Stroh, the grandson of Stroh's founder, Bernhard, sold insurance before he applied for a brewing license in 1933. Due to declining health, Edwin's father sold his interest in the brewery to his younger brother, Julius. Edwin apparently saw this as a time and place to reenter the industry and planned for a space in Dearborn on Schaefer Road. He went to the top industrial architect in the city, Albert Kahn Engineering, with plans for a 200,000-barrel brewery. It was to be tall, with strong, vertical lines for the brewhouse, along with a two-story building for offices and a low building for packaging.

Stroh then contacted Hiram Walker Ltd. for financing and met with Harrington E. Walker, who liked the idea so much that he assumed control from Stroh, announcing the organization of H.E. Walker Distillers and Brewers Inc. in January 1934. The new company planned to distill nine thousand gallons on a site, next to the future Fort Dearborn Brewing

Company. A board of luminaries quickly formed, including James Vernor Jr., Fritz Goebel, Bernhard Stroh (Edwin's brother), Edwin and Albert Kahn. Despite this group of talented and well-heeled men, the final plan was never realized. Hiram Walker pondered building the distillery in Detroit but then dropped out completely.

A separate entity formed in 1936 with the idea of building a brewery on the original site. Edwin Stroh again took the reins as president, but without Walker's backing, the funds did not materialize, and Edwin's window of opportunity closed before the dream could be realized.

Blum's *Brewing in Detroit* book states that it is possible the investors realized that demand was being met by existing breweries and therefore did not move quickly enough to get the brewery built. He later opines that it is entirely likely that the teetotaler Henry Ford did not want a distillery in his backyard. The book's author, Blum, wrote, "One can only imagine what transpired," and indeed, that is what we are left with, as evidence confirming or denying this could not be found.

WYANDOTTE

Wyandotte is now home to a large BASF plant, but earlier in its existence, it boasted Eureka Iron Works, the first mill in the country to produce steel using the Bessemer process. It has long enjoyed a boat club and a lovely waterfront. In its early days, the town was not really known for its beer, as only two breweries existed there prior to Prohibition.

George Marx started brewing at Front and Oak Streets in 1863, later bringing in his brothers and son. In 1884, the company's name was changed to Marx Brothers Brewing Company, and two years later, it added a dance hall and expanded to fill the entire block on Front Street. Its brands included Export, Pilsener and White Label.

In 1890, Eureka Brewing and Ice Company was opened on Front Street by Charles Riopelle and Hugo Mehlhose. After two decades, it began to fail, and the interests were sold to the Marx family—Eureka Brewing closed. The company picked up on growing prohibition sentiment and began making nonalcoholic drinks called Marxie and MaltJuice. When Prohibition began, it could not compete with the real beer from Canada, but its ice business remained profitable.

Marx Brewing barge. *Courtesy of the Detroit Public Library.*

Marx's brewing garage of vehicles, just waiting to make deliveries. *Courtesy of the Detroit Public Library.*

In November 1933, the Marx brewery reopened. By the next year, over forty-three thousand barrels were being brewed there annually. The good times lasted until 1936, when internal friction led to the brewery's closure. Its assets were auctioned off in the summer of 1937, and the building was razed four years later.

WASHTENAW COUNTY

Manchester

The village of Manchester has a lovely downtown area, with scenic parks and a historic gazebo. In the early part of the twentieth century, it had a different reputation—that of the "wettest city" in the lower part of Michigan. By 1870, the Raisin River Dams powered mills, factories and foundries. It also boasted two breweries, a distillery and seven saloons. Despite being among an ever-growing temperance movement, they did good business, welcoming German immigrants and American-born drinkers alike—and refusing to sign the pledge not to sell alcoholic drinks like the temperance movements wished.

The first brewery was located near the Duncan Street Bridge and was started by the father of Newman Granger, who was also the first council president of the village. Newman took over as the company's proprietor in 1870. The brewery went by several names during its existence, including Granger and Morgan, Granger and Strickland and Lawrence Traub's Brewery.

Over at 606 South Macomb Street, the Michigan Southern Brewery ran from 1871 through Prohibition. Its initial proprietors were John Baur from Germany and Henry Einbeck. Baur ran the brewery, which specialized in German lagers, until late 1873, when he sold to Christian Renz and Albert Eckerle, both from Indiana.

The brewery saw its biggest period of growth under the leadership of John Koch, between 1884 and 1892. Koch was born in Bavaria in 1840 and came to America at the age of twenty-five. He began his brewing career with the Ulmer Lager Beer Brewery behind his Detroit home. After he sold that operation, he came to Manchester and quickly began improving Michigan Southern Brewery. In 1887, the Manchester Bottling Works Company moved to the brewery, allowing Koch to sell beer by the keg, barrel and bottle. Getting ice from the River Raisin proved to be a sticking point for Koch and his brewery, as the other local merchants were also in need. In 1890, Koch leased a small lake south of the village and used a fire engine pump to send additional water to the surface to improve his ice quantities.

Note: The Manchester Enterprise *reported on the German Day Parade in 1891, saying that it featured a wagon carrying two large barrels that read "KOCH'S LYMPH."* Lymph *was a medical treatment developed by another Koch—Dr. Robert Koch (a cousin of John Koch)—that promised to find, cure and prevent tuberculosis. The paper opined that perhaps John Koch saw this opportunity to intimate that his lager beer might also provide health benefits for those who enjoyed it. Alas, Dr. Koch's Lymph did detect tuberculosis, but it neither cured nor prevented it.*

John Koch passed away in 1892 at the age of fifty-one. His son arrived in town to take over the operations, but John's widow and daughter opted to sell the property. The new owners made improvements, including the installation of a salt brine pump and cooling machine to reduce the company's reliance on the River Raisin for ice. The brewery carried on with success, but by the early 1900s, it saw a growing movement for prohibition. In 1907, its ownership changed hands again, and the business was renamed the Manchester Brewing Company.

Temperance gave way to Prohibition at the end of the nineteenth and beginning of the twentieth centuries. Manchester hung onto its "wettest city" designation, despite surrounding areas moving toward going "dry." Both Lenawee and Jackson Counties went dry—along with other lower peninsula counties—in 1909 and 1910. After statewide prohibition went into effect, brewers and saloons tried to keep going with near beer, but all except for Sloat's Saloon had closed by 1920.

The Manchester Brewing Company's building burned down on June 24, 1920.

Ann Arbor

Ann Arbor, the county seat of Washtenaw County, home of the University of Michigan and consistently ranked as one of the best cities in which to live also has a long history of beer brewing.

By 1861, there were three breweries in Ann Arbor: Hooper's (located at State and Fuller Streets from 1858 to 1866), the Bavarian (which operated on

Fuller Street, between Elizabeth and State Streets, from 1860 to 1872) and the City Brewery. The former two were considered small home operations, but the City Brewery was larger and more commercially successful.

A fourth brewery soon entered the scene. The Western Brewery was started by Peter Brehm at 416 Fourth Street in 1861. His focus was on lager, and the appetite for this light beer made Brehm a wealthy man. He purchased land at 326 West Liberty Street and built a mansion in the Second Empire style; the building still stands today.

Things ran smoothly until the Panic of 1873 hit. Banks failed, the New York Stock Exchange closed for ten days, businesses laid off employees and railroad construction and new building efforts stopped. Many breweries, both locally and nationwide, were caught up in the economic depression; however, the Western Brewery continued, albeit under different ownership.

It is not known why Brehm lost ownership of his brewery just before the panic; however, it is known that he suffered from what the newspapers described as "mania" or "melancholy." Tragically, Brehm came home one day in 1873, told his wife he was being sued and left home for downtown Ann Arbor. Later, he returned to his room and died from a self-inflicted gunshot wound to the head. Newspaper reports were kind to Brehm, saying he was "a kind-hearted and very generous man, respected by all who knew him."

After Brehm's death, Christian Martin and Matthias Fischer bought Western Brewery, keeping the name and carrying on the business of brewing beer. In 1903, new owners took over and renamed it the Michigan Union Brewery, as most of the employees were represented by a local union. By 1906, it was the last brewery left in town and even made it through Prohibition. The owners rented an ice cream maker and churned out sweet, cold treats for customers. Once Prohibition ended, three partners, including Peter Brehm's son Gustave, took over and reopened as the Ann Arbor Brewing Company.

Ann Arbor Brewing's Old Tyme label.
Courtesy of Stephen Johnson.

Customers could go into the back of the brewery, fill up a stein

Ann Arbor Brewing's Cream Top beer label. *Courtesy of Stephen Johnson.*

and drink a beer for free. They could choose from Cream Top Ale, Old-Tyme Ale and Town Club; however, these were all the same beer. The only different ale the brewery produced was a springtime bock. While the beer was described by at least one resident as being only good to put out fires with, the brewery nevertheless remained open until 1949.

During the original Western Brewery operations, two other directionally named brewpubs were also in business. In 1872, the Northern Brewery opened at 1037 Jones Drive, and in 1865, the Central Brewery began operations at 724 North Fifth Avenue. Northern operated until 1909, and Central operated until 1875.

Situated on Traver Creek, Northern Brewery was opened by George Krause in 1872. Twelve years later, Herman Hardinghaus took over the brewery, adding a new brick structure for his endeavors, as well as a brewmaster's house next door. After Hardinghaus left the business to become a partner in Ypsilanti's L.Z. Foerster & Company, Ernest Rehberg brewed beer there until about 1908, when he converted it to an ice business. The building now houses the Tech Brewery, a coworking space.

Central Brewery made beer until the late 1870s, at which time, breweries all over the country were declining in number. The economic depression after the financial panic, combined with local prohibition laws, forced many brewers to close up shop. The Central Brewery building later became the Ann Arbor Pop Works, where Bert Stoll made ginger ale and root beer; it then served as home to Ross and Welch's Bottling Works. After that, the building at 724 North Fifth Avenue housed German immigrants, Italian immigrants and, later, Japanese Americans released from detainment camps after the end of World War II. It is now an apartment complex called Brewery Apartments.

Ypsilanti

As early as the 1860s, Ypsilanti had two brewers in town. One was Jacob F. Grobe, who was born in 1839 in Meckleburg, Germany, and immigrated to America with his parents at the age of twelve in 1851. He first settled with his family in Monroe and then moved to Detroit to apprentice with a brewer named John Gredinger. He came to Ypsilanti in 1861 and married Sophie Post.

Note: In most historical recollections, his name is spelled "Grob." However, the Ypsilanti Gleanings *fall 2017 issue indicates that his name was actually Jacob Grobe. It was misspelled in the* History of Washtenaw County *(1881), and the incorrect spelling was copied thereafter.*

Grobe's brewery is credited as being the first in town. He built it at his house on Forest Street the same year he arrived in town; in 1864, he built the village's first icehouse. By late 1870s, his home was operating both as a brewery and a saloon. By the late 1880s, he was exclusively working with his ice business.

Grobe's ice company provided tons of ice to the city in the hot summer months. In the winter of 1880–81 he harvested over six hundred cords (four by four by eight feet) of ice. The Peninsular Ice Company sold ice until 1918, when a shop that made ice with electricity opened on Huron Street.

According to *Gleanings*, Jacob continued to brew until at least the 1900s, but by 1910, at the age of seventy-one, he was no longer listed as a brewer. It is noted that both his age and the competition from the Foerster Brewery likely weakened the business. Jacob died in 1921 at the age of eighty-three, and he was buried in Highland Cemetery.

Jacob Grobe with his ice wagon need. *Courtesy of the Ypsilanti Historical Society Archives.*

Other breweries of that era included the Eagle Brewery, located on East Congress Street from 1866 to 1876, and Swayne's Malt House located at Forest Avenue and River Street from 1870 to the 1890s. Grocer Andrew J. Leech changed occupations to become a brewer, and L.C. Wallington turned a schoolhouse into a malting operation, malting forty thousand bushels by 1880.

Foerster

Adam Foerster apprenticed at an Ontario brewery before becoming a brewery salesman in Cincinnati, while his brother Louis Z's (sometimes known as L.Z.) trade was carpentry. Both brothers arrived in Ypsilanti in 1870 and bought a small frame brewery on Grove Street at Prospect Street. (Some listings indicate the exact address as 414 South Grove Street.) The brewery was originally started by a Mr. Taulkirth and Mr. Trockenberg, who called it the Grove Brewery and Bottling Works and made about fifty barrels a year.

After changing the name to Adam Foerster & Brothers and increasing the production, the brothers sought out the finest local ingredients to make beer. They bought their malt from the local Swaine Malt House and used water from Louis's farm well. In 1874, Adam moved on to a brewery in Indiana and then to Lansing, where he built a large brewery.

This 1912 picture of brewers from Louis Z's brewery was taken by a twelve-year-old worker named Michael Sullivan. Michael's job was to have a bucket of beer ready to fill the empty drinking vessels of the workers. *Courtesy of the Ypsilanti Historical Society Archives.*

In the meantime, Louis owned the business on his own until Herman Hardinghaus joined him as a partner. Operating under the name L.Z. Foerster & Company, the brewery thrived, with sales growing to about five thousand barrels a year within five years. Louis added on to the original brewery, built a barn to house delivery wagons and horses and even added a bottling works across the street. In 1890, three of his sons, Louis K., Jacob, and Albert, joined him in the family business. When he was fifty-six, Louis went to Chicago to attend the American Brewing Academy, studying math, physics, chemistry, biology and bacteriology before eventually graduating with a master's degree in the art of brewing. The brewery's Pilsner, "Gold Band Export," and his its were shipped all over the state of Michigan.

In 1914, the L.Z. Foerster Brewing Company was sold to the Hoch Brewing Company. It was then empty until it became known as the Liberty Brewing Company from 1933 to 1934. After that, it was turned into the Ypsilanti Brewing Company for a year and was then known as the Chris Vogt Ypsilanti Brewing Company from 1935 to 1941 and finally the Dawes

Brewing Company from 1941 to 1943. In that final year, its doors closed for good, and its equipment was sold to Altes Brewing in Detroit.

Louis Z. lived to the age of eighty-five and was buried in Highland Cemetery.

Vogt

Vogt's Beer label for his German lager. *Courtesy of Stephen Johnson.*

Christopher Vogt owned the Ypsilanti Brewing Company from 1934 to 1941, brewing a beer called Old Ypsilanti. Vogt sold the company in 1941 to Detroit investors, who reopened it as Dawes Brewing Company. Unfortunately, it couldn't establish itself due to wartime restrictions and only existed until 1943. Ultimately, the company's equipment was purchased by the Altes Brewing Company in Detroit, and the building was razed, thus ending the local brewing scene for many decades to come.

MACOMB

Mount Clemens

Mount Clemens is now the bustling county seat of Macomb, but at one time, it was known for being a health resort town. While it was not known as a beer destination, it did attract enough relaxation seekers to support breweries in pre-Prohibition Michigan. William Miller brewed lagers and wheat beers on Front Street from 1860 to 1884. August Biewer brewed at the Clinton River Brewery from 1873 to 1919 while running a saloon on Court Street and the Biewer Gardens on South Gratiot Avenue. One can see by the date of its closing that Prohibition was the cause of the demise of the brewery. The Biewer family moved to St. Clair, where they owned and operated the Sherman House.

Mount Clemens Brewing Company existed from 1890 to 1935. Known for its Pearl Foam Beer, it operated at 37 South Front Street, near the Clinton River; a tunnel for aging beer exited to the Clinton River's bank. During

Mount Clemens Brewing Company. *Courtesy of the Detroit Public Library.*

Prohibition, the company's owner John Freimann attempted to keep the brewery open by making soft drinks, "near beer" and cider; however, this endeavor failed. In 1933, Freimann's son, widow and stepson reopened the brewery. When the brewmaster left for another opportunity, the company's operations ceased, and it declared bankruptcy in 1934.

OAKLAND COUNTY

Milford

The town of Milford appears to have had at least one brewery in the late 1800s. J. Brielmaier advertised in the December 21, 1872 issue of the *Milford Times* that his new brewery would "use none but the best of materials and will warrant my beer strictly pure and healthful." He also said he would have yeast "constantly on hand for sale." The paper added that Brielmaier had a "large experience in the business" of brewing.

Oxford

Oxford boasted Findon's Brewery, located at Broadway and Depot Streets, that was opened in 1876 and closed in 1885. The brewery made five hundred barrels a year, mostly to supply Findon's Saloon and hotel guests with beer. A 1977 article in the *Oxford Leader* reported that William Findon likely also acted as the "local party store" of his era, as beer was sold by the "tinful," with people bringing their tins to the saloon, filling up and taking them home with them.

William passed away in 1902, but his wife, Lottie, went on to live until she was 110 years old, becoming the oldest resident in the county. Born in 1847, Lottie came to Oxford from Birmingham, England, and married William when she was 18 years old. After marrying William, she worked as a cook in his tavern. Lottie Findon had lived in Oxford for 100 years at the time of her passing. (It is interesting to note that Mildred Schmidt, the curator of the local historical museum, indicated that she had very few notes on the brewery because "people only got mentioned in the histories for a fee.")

Pontiac

Brewing in Pontiac began in the 1850s, when Robert Dawson brewed on Saginaw Street. Like many of the early homebrewers, he established himself at his residence. By the late 1870s, he was brewing about three hundred barrels a year. The last directory information about him was from 1886, when his operation was listed opposite "Dawson's Exchange," indicating that he was doing more than just brewing.

The 1870s also saw James Carhartt brewing on Patterson Street. One of Pontiac's earliest residents, Carhartt was a grocer who ventured into beer brewing with at least three of his relatives. The largest brewery before Prohibition was Pontiac Brewing Company at 36–40 Patterson Street. Raymond Clemens originally incorporated the business in 1900, reincorporating in 1905 with new financial backing. Its brands included Pontiac Favorite and Blue Label, with the slogan "the beer that made Milwaukee jealous." It ran until 1915.

Wolverine beer label. *Courtesy of Stephen Johnson.*

After Prohibition, the Wolverine Brewing Company incorporated, with operations at 555 Going Street. A year after opening, the brewery was churning out almost forty thousand barrels a year. One notable beer was called "Dark Horse Ale," and another was called "The Aristocrat" (this beer was reportedly based on a formula that won at the 1893 Chicago World's Fair). The wartime restrictions of World War II proved challenging, and operations ceased in 1943.

5

THE NEW WAVE

Brewpubs and microbreweries began appearing on the West Coast in the early 1970s. This attention to small batches, local ingredients and quality products was a bit of a throwback to the early days, when brewing small with local grain and hops was just the way things were done. In Michigan, this "new wave" of beer began in the 1980s.

The first new wave brewery to open in the state was the Real Ale House Co. Inc. in Chelsea. Ted Badgerow and Gordon Averill raised over $12,000 to launch their brewery in the historic clocktower in the downtown area. Licensed in 1982, it was one of only forty-one brewing companies in the United States; only Stroh and Frankenmuth were brewing in Michigan. The brewers were not allowed to sell their products on site, but they were able to give samples and sell offsite to the tune of $20 per case ($6 less than the cost to make them). The brewery stopped production in 1984 and sold the brew kettle (a fifteen-gallon soup pot) to Larry Bell. Badgerow is now the co-owner of Mishigama Brewing Company, which opened in 2015 as the Ypsi Alehouse.

That soup pot was quickly put to good use. Larry Bell had taken a $200 birthday gift from his mother, incorporated the Kalamazoo Brewing Company, and set up a homebrew supply store on Burdick Street in downtown Kalamazoo. Its first beer, brewed out of that fifteen-gallon soup pot he got in Chelsea, was sold on September 19, 1985. The next year, the production reached 135 barrels, all of which was distributed by Bell

Original Bell's growler. *Courtesy of Bell's Brewery.*

and his staff. In 1989, the Ann Arbor–based wholesaler Rave Associates spread Bell's beer around the state, as more than 500 barrels were shipped annually. In June 1993, Bell's (still known as the Kalamazoo Brewing Company) became the first Michigan brewery to open its own on-site pub called the Eccentric Café. In 2006, the company legally changed its name to Bell's Brewery Inc., and it continues its enormous success to this day as one of the largest craft breweries in the nation, producing more than 500,000 barrels a year.

By 1988, only Bell and the Kalamazoo Brewing Company, Stroh Brewery, the Frankenmuth Brewery and the G. Heileman Brewing Company were making beer in the state of Michigan. But things were about to change.

FOUNDERS

A longtime staple of Grand Rapids, Founders Brewing Company began its life as the John Pannell Brewing Company. When Mike Stevens and Dave Engbers founded the business in 1996, they consciously located it in downtown Grand Rapids. As *Brewed in Michigan* states, the recent college graduates wanted to be part of the culture of their hometown; in doing so, they wholly changed the nature of downtown Grand Rapids.

In the latter part of the twentieth century, the city was facing the same problems that many other larger cities were facing—lack of investment, dwindling population and troubled infrastructure. Along came the brewery in 1997, then called the Canal Street Brewing Company. Its original location was on Monroe Street (once known as Canal Street), the home of other breweries a century or more before. Some of its first beer labels featured a historic picture of four brewers sitting on a wooden beer barrel with the name "Founders" above it. Customers started calling it Founders, leading Stevens and Engbers to adopt the name for common use. A customer designed a new label in exchange for free beer, and the logo has been around ever since.

While Founders is a shining star today, there were some early struggles. Renovations to the space on Monroe Street took longer than anticipated. The Robert Thomas Brewing Company, another new brewery in Grand Rapids, sued for an injunction to stop the company from advertising as a Grand Rapids Brewery, because their beer was brewed in Minnesota. (The judge denied the injunction, wisely noting that this would be a moot point once they began brewing in Grand Rapids, which they planned to do once renovations were complete).

Stevens and Engbers bartended at the Founders Taproom when it opened in 1998, living off of their tips when sales lagged. In 2000, Founders hovered on the brink of bankruptcy, and its landlord warned that he would bolt the doors unless rent was paid. The company was turning out pale ales, ambers and wheat beers that it described as "unremarkable." In a 2012 interview with MLive, cofounder Engbers said that the company had found its "sweet spot…[and] started talking about making the beers we liked to drink."

Thanks to a phone call to the bank by the late Peter C. Cook, a Grand Rapids benefactor and businessman, the brewery's doors stayed open. A change in philosophy followed, as the brewers decided that Founders beer would be "brewed for us," changing to unfiltered beer—bold, big-bodied and with rich flavors. In the early 2000s, barrel-aged Kentucky Breakfast Stout and Dirty Bastard appeared on draft. Customers responded to the better beer, and sales improved.

Founders moved to Grandville Avenue in 2007, expanding its market to thirty-seven states and 340,000 barrels a year. Its subsequent beers included Red's Rye IPA, All-Day IPA, Rubaeus, Backwoods Bastard and Bolt Cutter, a barley wine and a nod to those early days.

The Spanish brewing company Mahou San Miguel bought a 30 percent stake in the business in 2015. Five years later, the company sold another 60 percent to Mahou, with the original founders each retaining a 5 percent share.

ATWATER

Atwater Brewery in Detroit. *Courtesy of Atwater Brewery.*

Opened as the Atwater Block Brewery in 1997, the company's original intent was to resurrect the Bohemian lager made famous by Stroh. To that end, the original owners bought equipment from Kasper Schulz, the world's oldest brewing equipment producers. They also moved their brewery and taproom into the warehouse directly across from where Stroh had its headquarters. Despite an original multimillion-dollar investment, they nonetheless saw financial struggles that resulted in the company's closure in 2000.

Fortunately, Mark Rieth was there to save the day. Rieth was a homebrewer who had moved back to Detroit the same year that Atwater had opened, quickly becoming a regular customer. He invested in the brewery in 2002 and got things up and running once again.

Rieth, who purchased the brewery outright in 2005, focused on brewing and distribution out of the warehouse, although there was eventually a small bar and tables for customers to drink on the premises. Despite their initial hesitations to open a taproom, in 2014, Rieth brought in BrauKon Brewing from Munich and converted a Grosse Pointe church into Atwater in the Park. The success of this venture led him to open a taproom and restaurant at the old Atwater Block's taproom on Joseph Campau Avenue in Detroit. Another location was added in Grand Rapids in 2016.

In 2020, Tenth and Black Beer Company, the "craft" division of Molson Coors Beverage Company, acquired Atwater. The local leadership team remained in place, retaining control over its products.

SHORT'S BREWING COMPANY

In 2002, a twenty-two-year-old brewer named Joe Short registered a new business. An empty, 120-year-old hardware store in Bellaire was refurbished a year later by Short and his friends. The furnishings and décor—from the tile to the trim—were revitalized by Short, his friends and volunteers. The group ran into roadblocks but was able to open the pub on April 26, 2004. Like others experienced, the pub's initial years were slow. Things started

Short's. *Courtesy of Short's Brewing Company.*

to pick up when Scott Newman-Bale joined the team, helping the company obtain financing for various projects.

In 2017, a 19.99 percent share was sold to the Heineken-owned Lagunitas Brewing Company. In 2020, Short's acquired the beer brands and intellectual properties of Arcadia Brewing Company, a Battle Creek–based brewery that went out of business in 2019.

DARK HORSE BREWING COMPANY

Dark Horse Brewing Company began its life as a restaurant in Marshall, Michigan. In 1997, when Aaron Morse came home to Marshall after graduating from college, he and his business partners opened a gastropub on Michigan Avenue. The restaurant featured both macrobrews and its own craft beer line. After the business closed in 2000, Morse moved the brewing equipment to where his father's defunct party store, Wacky Willy's, was located. This time, he focused on the beer, and success followed.

The History Channel featured a reality show called *Dark Horse Nation* in 2014. That same year, the brewery ranked sixth in the state for production by volume.

In 2019, Royal Oak's ROAK Brewing Company acquired Dark Horse in what was described as a merger in a 2019 *Detroit Free Press* article. Aaron Morse retained his owner's interest, and the two companies share both personnel and financial resources.

JOLLY PUMPKIN ARTISAN ALES

Perhaps one of the truest statements in beer comes directly from Jolly Pumpkin's website: "founder Ron Jeffries has forgotten more about sour beer than most humans will ever know."

In the early 1990s, Jeffries began his study of the science of brewing and began brewing professionally in 1995. Jolly Pumpkin quickly gained a reputation for outstanding beer. The name came about because it made Ron and Laurie Jeffries happy, encompassing "everything we wanted to express about the brewery" (this information was taken from the company's website). The words "artisan ales" described the mission and plans of the brewery—to create the best beers of artisanal quality by retaining small-scale production and dedicating themselves to the craft of creating a perfectly balanced beer.

All of the company's beers are aged in oak, including barrels that once held wine and bourbon. The cultures in the wood create the complex flavor of the beers, described as everything from wild, funky and earthy—and occasionally, "sweaty horse character." The beers trend toward farmhouse or wild ales and have won multiple awards since the inception of the brewery. Currently, the brewery operates seven pubs around the state of Michigan.

RIGHT BRAIN BREWERY

In 2007, Russell Springsteen opened Right Brain Brewery in Traverse City. At the same time, he continued to operate his hair salon, Salon Saloon. In the years since he moved locations, he has relocated the salon (it is now connected to the brewery at 225 East Sixteenth Street) and grown to produce 1,800 barrels a year (as of 2017).

Right Brain is fearless when it comes to beer. No extracts are used, which means that its asparagus beer, Girl Scout Thin Mint Cookie beer, cherry pie beer and Mangalitsa pig porter beer all contain real ingredients. Its unique approach to beer lends to its continued success in Traverse City's SoFo neighborhood.

BLACKROCKS BREWERY

The founders of Blackrocks initially agreed to run a nano brewery (1 BBL brewhouse). Homebrewers David Manson and Andy Langlois were both facing downsizing at their jobs as pharmaceutical reps so in 2010, so they took the plunge. Locals discovered the beers being made at the pub on Third Street in Marquette, and their small-batch brews sold out quickly. Manson and Langlois soon extended operations to a 3-barrel system. In 2013, Blackrocks bought a former nine-thousand-square-foot bottling plant, installed a 20-barrel system and grew production to 4,500 barrels a year. They added an extension to the bottling plant in 2018 and two 120-barrel fermenters two years later.

Customers can enjoy the brewery's beer in its original location on Third Street, a space that was once a residential home. Additional structures were purchased in 2020 to expand seating and event space.

It is one of the largest breweries in the Upper Peninsula, reaching into Wisconsin and all of Michigan.

Blackrock's. *Courtesy of Blackrocks Brewery.*

CHANGING THE LAW

Ben Edwards was a high school English teacher who bought a bar in the Cass Corridor in 1965, turning it into the Traffic Jam and Snug. The establishment thrived, beloved by everyone from college professors to suburbanites visiting the city. Edwards' bakery and dairy provided cheese and bread, and he wanted to add something that would complement these homemade treats—on-site-brewed beer. But that was not allowed. At the time, Michigan law prohibited a restaurant from owning a license to sell beer and a license to brew beer.

According to *Brewed in Michigan*, Edwards built a small, ten-barrel system on his property and then asked the Michigan Liquor Control Commission (MLCC) for a brewery license for his restaurant. The MLCC denied Edwards' request to become the state's fifth brewery. That's where Thomas Burns Jr. enters the picture.

Tom Burns Jr. worked for a brewing company in Oregon while he was a law student, and then he practiced law in Colorado. He returned to Michigan, where and he and Edwards stepped forward to challenge Michigan's liquor law, asserting that it was contrary to the Sherman Antitrust Act. They lost their federal court cases, so in 1992, they sued the state in state courts. They got as far as the court of appeals, which ruled that it was a matter for the legislature.

Fortunately, Burns and Edwards had already begun working to change the law through legislation. State Representative Curtis Hertel Sr., a regular patron of the Traffic Jam, was working for them. Hertel introduced a bill in 1990, asking that restaurants be allowed to sell beer made on the premises. Opposed by the Michigan Beer and Wine Wholesalers Association, the proposed bill died in committee.

The next year, Hertel pressed on and entered negotiations with the powerful wholesalers' association, which demanded a cap on how much beer any one brewpub could produce in a year and a requirement that any beer produced must be distributed through a distributor (the "three-tier system"). It wasn't perfect, but it did become law on December 8, 1992, when the Michigan state legislature passed Public Act 300, allowing restaurants and microbreweries to brew their own beer and serve it by the glass on-site.

Almost immediately, things began to happen in Michigan. The Traffic Jam got the first license, the Grand Rapids Brewing Company got the second, Dean Wiltse from Oscoda got the third and Escanaba's Hereford and Hops got the fourth. Plans were made to open the Grizzly Peak and

Arbor Brewing Company in Ann Arbor, and Larry Bell made plans to open his taproom.

In addition to those previously mentioned, some other early "new wave" breweries were: Arcadia Ales, Atwater Brewery, New Holland, Dark Horse, Mackinac Brewing, Founders (then called John Pannell Brewing Company), the Big Rock Chop & Brew House, C.J.'s Brewing Company, Big Buck Brewery & Steakhouse, Copper Canyon Brewery, Detroit Brew Factory, Dragonmead Microbrewery, Fire Academy Brewery and Grill, Local Color Brewing Company, O'Mara's Restaurant & Brewpub, Royal Oak Brewery and Woodward Avenue Brewers. Other early ventures included: King Brewery, Bo's Brewery & Bistro, Bad Frog, Bear River Brewing, Traverse Brewing Company, Blind Tiger, Frog Island, Duster's Microbrewery and the Michigan Brewing Company, Leopold Brothers, Brewbakers Craft Brewery and Bakehouse, Great Baraboo, Rochester Mills, Roffey Brewing Company/ Robert Thomas Brewing Company, Arena Brewing Company, the B.O.B., the Olde Peninsula Brewpub & Restaurant, the Blue Coyote, Harper's Brew Pub and the Lansing Brewing Company.

Many of these early ventures do not exist anymore. While writing of this book, the COVID-19 pandemic struck. Not since Prohibition and perhaps World War II has a single event so affected this beloved industry. Countless breweries had to pivot to something new—curbside refreshments, carryout food, crowlers, howlers, canning, social distancing, mandatory closures, cocktails to go and so on.

Not everyone made it. But despite these setbacks, the industry carries on in Michigan. As of the writing of this book, there are well over three hundred breweries in Michigan, with many more to come. And that is something we can all drink to.

ABOUT THE AUTHOR

Current special education teacher and former legal aid lawyer Patti F. Smith is the author of three nonfiction books: *Vanishing Ann Arbor*, *Downtown Ann Arbor* (Images of America) and *A History of the People's Food Co-op Ann Arbor*. She is also the author of one novel. She has written for CraftBeer.com, *Washtenaw Jewish News*, *West Suburban Living* magazine, Concentrate, Mittenbrew, *The Ann*, AADL's *Pulp* blog and the *Ann Arbor Observer*. Patti is a frequent public speaker around town, curating *HERsay* (an all-woman variety show), Grown Folks Reading (story time for grownups), *May It Please the Court?* (an all-lawyer show), Desserts by the Decade (food history program) and she tells stories at Ignite, Nerd Nite, Tellabration and Telling Tales Out of School. Patti serves as a commissioner for the Recreation Advisory Commission; is a teacher of history for Rec & Ed, a storyteller in the Ann Arbor Storytellers' Guild and a DJ for WCBN; and she volunteers for the Ann Arbor Film Festival. Patti lives with her husband, Ken Anderson, and dog, Pugsley Anderson-Smith, in Ann Arbor, Michigan. She loves a good Pilsner in the summer, an Oktoberfest in the fall and stouts all year round.

Visit us at
www.historypress.com